COMPUTER NETWORKING THE COMPLETE GUIDE:

A Complete Guide to Manage Computer Networks and to Learn Wireless Technology, Cisco CCNA, IP Subnetting and Network Security

ERICK STACK

Table of Contents

Introduction

Over the years, networking has gained immense popularity among the people as a result of the numerous benefits that can be reaped from computer networking. As more and more people are aware of the benefits of networking and reap the benefits, the technology will continue to experience increased popularity.

Some of the most popular benefits of networking, in no particular order, are:

Connectivity: The essence of networking is to connect computers and other devices together. With LAN, individuals within a workgroup or a building can easily be connected. Once users are connected, they can easily communicate with each other without delay through some technologies such as e-mail. Thus, business transactions, school discussions, and other issues can easily be communicated with each other without having to be physically present at a spot for the discussion.

Data sharing: Data sharing is one of the several uses of networking. Prior to the advent of networking, data sharing was expensive, inconvenient, and time-consuming. For instance, before the networking era, an employee who wanted to share a file with his or her boss will prepare the file on his or her PC, save it on a floppy disk or any other storage device, and take it to the manager who will also transfer the data to his or her PC.

You can imagine the amount of time and resources invested in that simple file-sharing process. You can do this in a couple of seconds with other networked computers. Thousands of employees can easily share data without going through the rigorous and time-consuming process I just described above. There is no need for them to plug a storage device into their system, copy numerous files, and walk over to whoever they want to or wherever the printer is before they can use the printer. More so, some applications, such as group software development, databases, and much more, require that many people have access to the same data.

Internet access: I once mentioned that the Internet is an example of a Wide Area Network. That's right. When you are surfing the net while looking for solution to an assignment, finding resources for a project, or just shopping, you are directly taking advantage of networked computers. We simply can't overemphasize the huge importance of the Internet in modern society. If you are in technical fields, you will understand the importance of the Internet better. This wouldn't be possible without networking.

Hardware sharing: The use of networking for sharing is not limited to data sharing alone. You can also leverage the technology for hardware sharing as well. For instance, if you have 100 employees, giving each one of them a printer will be quite expensive and may take a toll on your finances. However, networking has removed such a huge burden on employers. You simply need to connect all the computers used by the employees to a single printer and give each of them access to the printer to use at any time. That's hardware sharing. It is less expensive, both in acquisition and maintenance.

Internet access sharing: This is another area where sharing is taken to the next level. If you are using a small computer network for your business, your employees can share an Internet connection. With the assistance of some special hardware, various individuals on the network can have the bandwidth of the connection shared according to their respective needs. Thus, an organization may just purchase a high-speed, although more expensive, connection rather than purchase a couple of slower, less expensive ones.

Data management and security: A network is also useful in a business environment as administrators can leverage it for a better management of their company's confidential data. Rather than have the data spread over tons of computers randomly as they are created by the users, the data can be saved on shared servers where they can be centralized so whoever needs the data can easily find it. This also allows the administrators to ensure regular backing up of the data. More so, some security measures can be put in place to restrict access to the data or any other critical information to authorized personnel only.

Improved storage volume and efficiency: After networking your business computers, you will have a new data storage technique. First, all the storage volume of the computers is available for use. For instance, if you have 50 computers for your business and each one of them has 2 terabytes of storage space, this automatically means that you now have 100 terabytes of space once the computers are networked. More so, if you have a huge file for the computer users, you only need to save the huge file on the central server while other users have access to it. Without networking your business computers, you have to copy the file and save it on each of the computers. That will consume more space than when the file is stored on a single system.

It is inexpensive: It won't cost you a small fortune to install networking software on your computer or any other device. Since the technology is also durable, you will gain more than whatever amount of money that you spend on the installation. You also don't need to replace the software regularly since that is not absolutely necessary.

It is the platform for building the ecosystem: The advent of networking opened the gate for creating of some other technologies in the ecosystem. Some of the technologies that are built on networks are:

Supercomputers: A supercomputer is a computer that works at the highest efficiency rate for computers. These computers are used for engineering and scientific applications where it is mandatory to do a huge amount of computation or where handling large database is a must. In some instances, a supercomputer is expected to perform both functions creditably well.

Although the invention of general-purpose graphics processing units (GPGPUs) and multi-core processors have made it possible for powerful machines to be adapted to personal uses such as GUP supercomputer and a desktop supercomputer, a supercomputer is expected to display exceptional performance. A typical supercomputer is the China-based TaihuLight computer. With a peak performance in excess of 120 petaflops and 40,60 64-bit RISC processors with each processor having 260 cores each, it is a powerful machine with an impressive performance. Supercomputers have found a wide range of uses. From being used for scientific purposes to code cracking, ballistics to simulating the capacity of nuclear weapons, they can be used in virtually all facets of the human economy. Of course, you shouldn't forget the Deep Blue, a supercomputer that defeated the former world chess champion, Garry Kasparov in 1997.

Internet of Things: According to TechTarget, "The Internet of Things (IoT) is a system of interrelated computing devices, mechanical and digital machines, objects, animals, or people that are provided with unique identifiers and the ability to transfer data over a network without requiring human-to-human or human-to-computer interaction."

The "thing," in this case, can be a farm animal with an implanted biochip transponder, an individual with a heart monitor implant, an automobile with a built-in sensor, and other practical uses. This technology has practical applications in building management, precision agriculture, energy, healthcare, transportation, while inventors are working hard to ensure it is applied in all the facets of humanity.

Internet banking: In the past, banking operations were conducted in banks only. Whether you want to cash a check or make a payment to another account, you must visit your local bank to make conduct the transaction. Thanks to Internet banking, you can conduct all your banking transactions without leaving the comfort of your home or office. Internet banking now allows you the luxury of viewing your account balance, making payments, transferring money between your accounts, viewing your transaction details, and setting up and managing your payments.

Distributed computing: Distributed computing refers to sharing resources among multiple systems that may be scattered in different locations. In distributed computing, multiple computer systems may work on a single problem. The problem is divided into different parts while the different computers solve each part of the problem. Once the computers are on a network, it is easy for them to communicate with each other and proffer a solution to the problem. If the concept is done properly, all the computers that make up the network will work together as a single entity.

The Internet: One of the simplest and most comprehensive definitions of the Internet is this one by Wikipedia: "The Internet is the global system of interconnected computer networks that use the Internet protocol suite (TCP/IP) to link devices worldwide. It is a network of networks that consists of private, public, academic, business, and government networks of local to global scope, linked by a broad array of electronic, wireless, and optical networking technologies."

You obviously are conversant with the different areas of application of this innovation. As a reminder, it is used for research purposes, sharing ideas, content management, and whatever else have you. Without computer networking, all these technologies would not be created. Thanks to it, we have a better ecosystem and look forward to more inventions that will make the world better in the future.

Chapter 1 Virtual Private Networks (VPNs)

An organization that needs to connect several sites could select from various kinds of WAN services such as Multi-protocol Label Switching (MPLS), frame relay, and leased lines. These services are often expensive. But another much affordable option is available to connect locations. Every site could be linked online through internet access technology such as 3G, 4G, WiMAX, cable, or DSL. Each site could send data to each other through public internet as WAN.

However, there's one flaw in using internet as WAN. The Internet is not as safe compared to other alternatives. To a great extent, the vulnerability of the Internet is mainly because of the fact that it is publicly accessible. You just need a computer with reliable internet access to launch an attack. Other WAN alternatives identified here are generally safe. For instance, to steal information flowing through leased lines, you need to manually tap into the line using specialized tools or be physically present at the network. These actions are prohibited by law, and it takes time, effort, and knowledge to perform.

The option to use the Internet as WAN can be enticing in spite of the safety issues. But there is one technology that can address this concern. Virtual Private Network (VPN) technology is more secure. You will also explore the two primary types of Secure Sockets Layer (SSL) and IP Security (IPsec).

Advantages of Using VPN Over WAN

- Below are the advantages of using VPN instead of WAN technologies in connecting different sites.

- VPNs are much affordable compared to WAN alternatives.

- VPNs are more secure compared to WAN alternatives and are now used even by companies and organizations with strict security policies such as banks, government agencies, and credit card companies.

- VPNs can be easily scaled and are more cost-effective to set up and maintain in several sites. Every location could select from several options of web connectivity.

Concepts behind VPNs

VPNs are used to transmit data from a private network to another private network through a public hub like the Internet, but with added encryption to secure the data. To put it simply, a VPN is a secured link between private networks through public network, typically through the World Wide Web.

VPNs have the following main features:

- *Data Integrity* – VPNs make certain that the information passing through the network are not modified in any form.

- *Replay Proof / Anti-Relay* – VPNs make certain that unauthorized users cannot make any modification in the information that will be transmitted between private networks.

- *Privacy / Confidentiality* – VPNs prohibit anyone in the middle of the network to access and view the data packets. The Internet is naturally not safe as data usually passes through devices and networks under various administrative controls. Even is a user can intercept data at any point in the network, they cannot read it because of the added encryption.

- *Authentication / Verification* – VPNs utilize authentication to make certain that the device at the destination site is the right device and not an attacker who is just imitating a device.

In essence, a VPS is a safe channel, typically known as the tunnel, between two devices or site points. The end points of the VPN add encryption to the whole of the original IP packet, which means that the contents of the original packet cannot be interpreted by any user who was even able to access the copy of the packet as it passes through the network. The end points of the VPN also append headers to the original packet encryption. The added headers involve fields, which permit VPN devices to do all their functions.

The Cisco Adaptive Security Appliance (ASA) can be used as a VPN. But there are other software and hardware products that you can use to create a VPN. Cisco products that are equipped with VPN functions are the following:

Cisco ASA

Cisco ASA is a dynamic device, which integrates different security functions such as VPN functions and firewall in one piece of hardware. All Cisco ASA models provide IPsec as long as you meet the licensing requirements to enable the VPN function.

Cisco Routers

All Cisco routers that are running on IOS software are equipped to support IPsec VPNs. You just need to use an IOS image with the proper feature set. Cisco 2900, Cisco 1900, Cisco 2800, and Cisco 1800 are all examples of Cisco routers with enabled VPN.

Cisco VPN Clients

Cisco provides both software and hardware VPN clients. For instance, the Cisco AnyConnect Mobility Security Client is an example of VPN client software, which can be used on tablets, smartphones, and laptops.

Types of VPNs

The two basic types of VPNs are Remote Access and Site to Site.

Remote Access VPN

A remote access VPN is similar to a circuit switched technology such as the Integrated Services Digital Network (ISDN) or dial up networks. This type of VPN fills the connection requirements of telecommuters, mobile users, or those who are working at home. Remote access VPNs link every host instead of the entire network, which is the case of Site to Site VPN.

In using a remote access, you need to install a VPN client software on every host. Each time the host needs to transmit data, the VPN client software will encrypt and encapsulate that data before sending it out to the gateway at the entrance of the destination network. The gateway at the destination network will read this packet similarly as it does for site to site VPNs.

Site to Site VPN

Site to Site VPNs link a whole network to another network. For instance, you cannot link a sub-department network to the network at a main office. Before, a Frame Relay connection or a private leased line is needed to link the sites. But with easily accessible and cost-effective high-bandwidth web connection nowadays, site to site VPNs could now replace Frame Relay and leased lines.

Site to Site VPNs are also categorized as extranet and intranet VPNs. Once a remote site of an organization links to the main office of the same organization, it is known as an intranet VPN. If a company links to a supplier, it is known as an extranet VPN. In technical viewpoint, these VPN types are similar, but you need to understand the distinction between the two as it is often covered in the CCNA exam.

In a Site to Site VPN, you need to install a VPN gateway at every site, which performs the decryption, encryption, and other functions in support of the hosts on the network. There are different devices, which you can configure to serve as a VPN gateway such as a VPN concentrator, firewall, router, or other security devices created by Cisco or other providers. The VPN encrypts and encapsulates the aggregate of all traffic that is going out from the hosts on the local network and sends it through the VPN tunnel through the internet to another VPN gateway at the destination site. Once the peer VPN gateway accepts the transmission, it will decrypt and de-capsulate the data packet and will relay it to the target host within the private network.

Encryption

Encryption is the core mechanism used to add security to the data packets and it is the fundamental framework in implementing VPNs. Basically, encryption conceals data so it cannot be interpreted by any unauthorized user. It is a proven method to secure data over an insecure channel such as the public Internet. Before discussing encryption in detail, let's learn some of the basic terms:

Encryption – the method of converting plaintext to cipher text. It involves the application of an algorithm, which utilizes a binary string or secret key to convert a simple data into a secret code.

Plaintext – the original information prior to encryption.

Cipher text – the concealed information after the encryption.

Hash Value – or simple known as hash refers to the binary number generated from the original data by using a certain mathematical formula. You need to calculate the hash value from the original information to specifically determine the data.

Decryption – The reverse method of encryption, which us utilized to revert back the encrypted information into its original form.

Algorithms Used in Encryption

There are three basic types of algorithms used in data encryption: hash function, symmetric key cryptography, and asymmetric key cryptography.

A hash function refers to a one-way mathematical function, which is utilized to create a specific hash value from the original information. You cannot reverse a hash function, so you cannot reconstitute the original information from the hash value even if you are aware of the hash function. It is often appended to the original message as the specific identifier of the message such as biometric registries.

A symmetric key cryptography includes one key, which is utilized for both encryption and decryption.

An asymmetric key cryptography involves two separate keys. One is used for encryption, while the other one is for decryption.

In the figure below, you can see a very common algorithm known as the Caesar cipher. This is the encryption technique used by Julius Caesar in obscuring his private messages. Every letter is shifted to the left or right in a specific number of positions. In order to encrypt and decrypt the data, the sender and receiver should be aware of the direction of the shift and the number of positions.

Caesar cipher with a right shift of four positions will look like this:

Plaintext: ABC DEF GHI JKL MNO PQR STU VWX YZ

Cipher text: GHI JKL MNO PQR STU VWX YZA BCD EF

Take note that modern encryption algorithms are far more advanced compared to the Caesar cipher and uses complex mathematical calculations, which can only be solved by computers. But still, the core principle of encryption stays the same.

Symmetric key cryptography is much faster because it doesn't need complex computational algorithms. It is ideal for encrypting tons of data such as information transmission through VPN links. It is also less intensive in terms of computations so it could pass through network devices even without the allocated hardware for cryptography. As such, symmetric key cryptography is used by common cryptography algorithms today such as Data Encryption Standard (DES), Triple Data Encryption Standard (3DES), and Advanced Encryption Standard (AES).

DES

DES is a common cryptographic algo, which uses a 56-bit key in order to encrypt 64-bit data blocks. However, DES is no longer regarded as a secure method, and so it is not recommended for use. The flaw in the protocol is mainly due to key size of only 56 bits.

3DES

3DES is an improved protocol of DES, which uses up to 168 bits (three 56-bit keys). It runs three passes of encryption process through the same data block. Basically, 3DES was derived from DES to increase the key length without the need to use another algorithm. 3DES can also encrypt 64-bit data, similar to DES, although it utilizes a 168-bit key. It is an ideal replacement protocol for DES algorithms.

AES

Also named Rijndael, AES is one of the most widely used cryptography algorithms nowadays. It offers more flexibility than DES and 3DES because it utilizes a variable key length and data block length. It could use any combination of key lengths of 256 bits, 192 bits, or 128 bits as well as data block lengths of 256 bits, 192 bits, and 128 bits. Gradually, AES is replacing the 3DES and the DES standards.

Asymmetric key cryptography utilizes two keys – one key is used for encrypting the plaintext while the other key is used for decrypting the cipher text. Every end user should be provided with a pair of private and public keys. The public keys are accessible through a key management structure. Meanwhile the private key is only accessible to the user and should be never revealed or exchanged to anyone.

Asymmetric key cryptography is often utilized in VPN key management process, even though this is not ideal for encrypting data because of the intensity of computations. Examples of asymmetric key algorithms are Diffie Hellman (DH) and RSA.

Diffie Hellman is used for switching keys over a channel that is not secure, between two users with no pre-information about each other. You can use the secret key extracted through the DH to encrypt succeeding messages using a symmetric key algorithm such as AES or 3DES. Take note that the DH algorithm is only used for secret key switching.

On the other hand, the RSA algorithms could be used for digital signatures, key exchange, and data encryption. Its name was derived from the surnames of its developers: Rivest, Shamir, and Adleman.

Hash Functions

Has functions are composed of mathematical formulae that you can use to calculate a fixed-length has value from the original plaintext. It is also known by other names such as single encryption, one-way encryption, message digest, and hash algorithm. You cannot reconstitute the original data from the hash value even if you are aware of the hash function. You can use the hash functions to build digital fingerprints of any kind of data, which is then added to the original data. Hash functions add data integrity, which ensures that the information has not been modified during the transmission. Message Digest (MD) and Secure Hash Algorithm (SHA) are two of the most popularly used hash functions today.

Chapter 2 Virtualization & Cloud Computing

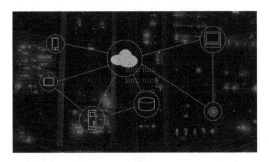

Today's modern datacenter is much different than it was 5-10 years ago, and is still evolving and changing at a rapid pace. With technology advancing so quickly, the days of the datacenter full of big clunky servers are over. Nowadays everything is being virtualized or run from "the cloud", allowing us to do more with less hardware.

Virtualization

Many modern datacenters are turning to a technology known as virtualization to downsize on the amount of physical servers that take up space, power, and financial resources. These physical servers are replaced with virtual servers that run within virtualization software installed on a physical server.

This hypervisor, as it's called, can be installed on supported physical servers, and then all these physical servers can be monitored from one management console. The management console can also monitor your VMs as well as your virtual infrastructure. There are several vendors that offer this type of platform that you can use in your environment. I will now discuss two of the biggest players in the game.

VMware

VMware has their flagship product called vSphere, and it's their enterprise level hypervisor capable of supporting thousands of VMs at multiple sites. You can run a variety of operating systems on their platform (including Windows, Linux, and Apple OS X) and used shared storage and networking resources to design the configuration you need for your business.

Their hypervisor is named ESXi and their management platform is called vCenter, and it's a web based management console that allows you to configure VMs, hosts, storage, networking, and other components. VMware also has other products to complement their vSphere product, such as cloud offerings and virtual desktops for end users.

Hyper-V

Microsoft has their own virtualization platform called Hyper-V, which runs on top of the Windows operating system. Hyper-V was first available with Windows Server 2008, and is still included with all the Windows Server releases. If you have Windows 8 or Windows 10, you can run a scaled down version of Hyper-V on your desktop. The only requirement is that your version of Windows must be a 64 bit edition running Professional, Enterprise, or Education.

Only Windows guest operating systems are supported on Hyper-V, but you can still run Linux with some limitations and lack of support. And since Hyper-V is included With Windows, all you need to do is enable the feature and you are ready to go (assuming you have the horsepower in your server to run multiple VMs and the storage available to assign to those VMs). Keep in mind that you need to pay for the Windows license, so it's not a totally free feature.

VirtualBox

I did want to mention one more virtualization product before we move on. If you want to play around with creating VMs at home and don't have the money to buy a VMware license or a Windows server license and don't have the right version of Windows 8 or 10, then a great solution to that problem is to use Oracle's VirtualBox virtualization software. It's free to use and fairly easy to understand and configure, and you will have your own virtual machines up and running in no time.

VirtualBox supports Windows, Linux, and Mac OS X guest operating systems, and you can use your locally attached hard drives as storage for those guests. You can install it on Windows, Linux, Macintosh, and Solaris operating systems.

Cloud Services

Another trend that has been taking off over the last several years is the concept of using cloud services for some or all of your IT infrastructure. This way all the hardware and configurations are stored at the cloud service provider's location and you access the things you need (such as file services or email servers) over the Internet rather than on your own local network.

By doing this companies can utilize resources as they need them rather than buying a bunch of hardware to install locally for huge amounts of money. Of course, with cloud services you are paying a monthly fee, but you also don't have to worry about being responsible for the infrastructure in case something breaks unless it's something tied to what you are using the resources for (such as your domain controller having a configuration issue).

There are various services you can use in the cloud, and they all have some fancy names such as Software as a Service (SaaS), Platform as a Service (PaaS), Infrastructure as a Service (IaaS), and Network as a Service (NaaS). Which service or services you decide to use will determine what you can do with these services.

- *SaaS* – This is the simplest type of cloud service because you only have control over the software that you are using and not things like the servers, network, storage, and so on. An example of SaaS would be Google Docs.
- *PaaS* – This is where you are given a platform to run your software on. You are not responsible for things like operating system maintenance, but you do have control over things like the servers, networking, and storage. An example of PaaS would be Microsoft Azure.

- *IaaS* – This cloud service level provides you with the most control over the resources that you are paying to use. You control the VMs, networking, storage, and so on, giving you the freedom to configure things the way you like while the service provider simply provides you with the means to do so. An example of IaaS would be Amazon Web Services.

- *NaaS* – NaaS is used when companies don't want to build their own network infrastructure on site and rely on the service provider to provide them with everything they need to get their network built and operational. This can reduce costs as well as the amount of time needed for your IT staff to maintain the network.

You can run your whole business in the cloud using their infrastructure (assuming you have the money to pay for it!). Both of them offer free trials, so if you want to get a taste of how cloud services work, you should check them out. Just be careful and watch your utilization because they will want to charge you once you go over your free limits, which really aren't much to begin with.

Home User Could Services

If you want to get a taste of how basic cloud services work, then you can get yourself a free cloud storage account. For most of them you can access your files via their website and also have a client on your computer that will sync your local files with your files in the cloud if that is what you are looking to do.

There are many companies that provide high level cloud storage with all sorts of options as to storage capacity and performance, but for the average home user or small business owner, you can stick with one of the "name brand" cloud providers and be just fine. Here is a list of the most commonly use ones:

- *DropBox* – DropBox has been around for years, and is probably the most commonly used basic cloud provider service. They will give you 2-5GB of free storage (depending on your plan), and then after that you will need to pay for an upgrade. The cost will vary depending on how much storage you need. The cheapest 1TB plan starts at $9.99\month.

- *Microsoft OneDrive* – Microsoft has gotten into the cloud storage game with its OneDrive software, which always seems to end up on your computer whether you asked for it or not. They have a 5GB free plan, and then they go up from there with the next level costing $1.99\month for 50GB. They have some pricier options that Include an Office 365 software subscription.

- *Google Drive* – Google offers you 15GB of free storage, and for $1.99\month you can upgrade to 100GB. The capacity and storage amounts go up from there.

- *Amazon Drive* – Amazon gives you 5GB of storage for free just for being an Amazon customer. If you are an Amazon Prime member, you get unlimited photo storage. For $11.99\year you can get 100GB of storage.

- *iCloud Storage* – Apple has their own cloud storage for all of your Apple devices such as your Mac, iPhone, and iPad, and you will get 5GB for free automatically. If you need additional storage, you can pay for it just like with the other cloud storage providers. For example, a 50GB plan will cost you $0.99 a month.

Chapter 3 Managing and Troubleshooting the Network

From time to time you will need to troubleshoot the network. You can have this done on schedule or on impulse, in response to an immediate threat. More often the need for troubleshooting catches you off guard. At times it is the very simple issues that make things difficult in the network. More often than not you worry about a serious problem, struggling to understand the cause, only to realize it was something simple, and perhaps all you needed was to reboot the network.

Network problems can overwhelm you. It gets worse when you have a problem at peak hours. Everyone on the network is unable to do their work until you sort out the problem. The pressure can be so intense, especially if you work in a fast-paced organization.

The first step in troubleshooting a network is to identify and narrow down the possibilities. The network issue might be caused by one of many reasons. Narrow them down and eliminate them one by one, especially if you cannot deduce an immediate cause.

For troubleshooting, no reason is ever too simple to be possible. Eliminate the possibility of a problem as a result of simple human errors. The following are the four key procedures that you should follow when troubleshooting a network concern:

- Check the network to ensure all the simple things are okay.

- Determine whether you have a software or hardware issue.

- Determine whether the issue is localized to the server or workstation.

- Find out the sectors in the network that are affected.

These four steps will help you eliminate possible causes one by one until you identify the problem, and fix it. Let's delve deeper into it.

Check the network to ensure all the simple things are okay

At times it is the simplest explanation that might solve your problem. Before you worry yourself about complex reasons for the network issue, try and eliminate any possibilities of a very small problem. Many are the times when someone will call you frantically that they are unable to access their account on the network, only to realize that they had the Caps Lock on.

While assessing the problem, ensure that the correct procedure is followed to access the network. Check to make sure the credentials are correct. Someone might be keying in the wrong details inadvertently. You'd be surprised the number of times people enter the wrong details and lock their accounts.

You can also create restrictions over the number of times users can sign into their devices. This alerts you when someone is struggling to access their accounts, and you can reach out and assist them accordingly. It might also come in handy and alert you when someone is trying to access a device they are not supposed to.

- Login problems

In case your network problem is user-oriented, ensure their login credentials are correct. Where possible, try to sign into the account from a separate workstation. In case that works try it on the problematic workstation to rule out any other challenges.

- Power connection

Check the power switch. Are all the devices that should be powered on running? There is always a risk that someone tripped on one of the cables and plugged it off the power source. You'd be surprised the number of times people complain about having a blank screen yet their computer is powered on, only to realize that the power cable to the screen was not plugged in correctly.

- Collision and link lights

Check the collision light and the link lights. The collision light blinks amber in color. You should see it on the hubs or the ethernet network interface card. If this light is on, you have a collision on the network. For a very busy network, collisions are very common.

However, if the light blinks frequently the collisions might be too much, affecting network traffic. Check to make sure the network interface card and any other network device are working properly, because one of them might have malfunctioned.

The link light is green in color. If the link lights are on for the network interface card and the hub where the workstation is connected, this is a sign that communication between the hub and workstation is not interfered with.

- Operator problems

Individual operators can have inhibitions that have nothing to do with the network, but lock them out and prevent them from accessing the network altogether. Perhaps the system you use is alien to the user. If they do not understand it, chances are high they will struggle to use it. Find out if the user has any challenges, and if so, walk them through it carefully so that they do not feel you undermine them or look down upon them.

Explain to them why they are experiencing the problem. Be firm and make the user confident to reach out whenever they have a similar problem or any other. If you do not inspire confidence in the user, they may shy away from informing you of a problem, and instead attempt to solve them on their own, which only makes things worse.

Determine whether you have a software or hardware issue

Hardware problems can be extreme. One of the devices might have outlived its useful life. Hardware problems might also mean you need to plan for data recovery or retrieval if the hardware fails. Fixes for hardware problems involve replacing the devices, updating device drivers or tweaking the device settings.

Troubleshooting software problems depend on the nature of the issue at hand. Most programs today are operated on a subscription basis. Perhaps the subscription has expired and was not renewed in good time, hence you are locked out of the system, or your user privileges have been limited to free user account terms. In such a case, follow up with the relevant parties and pay the subscription fee to restore full access.

Remember that whether you are dealing with a hardware or software issues, you might need to back-up your data. Ensure you have sufficient space for this.

Determine whether the issue is localized to the server or workstation

Identifying the extent of the problem can help you know how severe it is. If it is a server problem, a lot of people will be affected, and you might have too much to deal with than if it was just one workstation.

For a workstation problem, you can try to sign into that account from a different workstation in the same work-group. If that works, you can trace all the necessary steps to fix the problem. Check the connections, the cable, the keyboard and so forth. Chances are high that the problem might be simple.

Find out the sectors in the network that are affected

Determining the sectors in the network that are affected by the problem is not going to be an easy task. There are many possibilities here. In case a lot of people on the network are affected, your network might be suffering from a network address conflict.

Check your TCP/IP settings to make sure that all IP addresses on the network are correct. The problem comes in when any two sectors in the network share a subnet address. This causes a duplication in IP errors, and it might take you a while to realize the problem. In case everyone on the network has the same problem, it could be an issue with a server to which they are all connected. This is an easy one to solve.

Check the cables

The way the network is set up could be causing you problems. If you have checked and realized everything else on the network is fine but the system is still down, you need to look at the cables.

Ensure all the cables are connected to their appropriate ports. Patch cables between wall jacks and your workstations might need replacing. Most of the time people step on the cables, wheel over them with their chairs and so forth. If cables are run across the office floor, you might need to replace these, and probably consider a better way of running cables.

There are several cable issues that you might be experiencing. Most of them are basic, but they are the foundation of your network, so you have to know about them. Here are some of the cabling issues you might experience:

- **Interference**

Computers are highly susceptible to signal interference. Radio transmitters and TV sets interfere with computers most of the time. These devices generate radio frequencies during transmission. To avoid this problem, ensure you use shielded network cables for the entire network.

- **Shorts**

A short circuit might be caused by a physical fault in the cabling network. Today there are special tools that you can use to locate the short. More often than not, you will need to fix or replace the cable.

- **Collisions**

If two devices on your network are communicating at the same time and on the same segment, there will be a collision. Collisions are possible if you are still using older ethernet networks, or hubs. Replace hubs in the workplace with switches where possible, because switches are intelligent and can help you prevent collisions on the network.

- **Echo**

An echo is an open impedance mismatch. With cable testing equipment, you will know whether your cables are completing the circuit or not. Test to identify a bad connection. In case you experience an echo on all the wires at the same place, you might have a cut cable that needs replacing. Today some special testing equipment can show the exact location of a cut even if the cables are set behind the wall.

- **Attenuation**

Attenuation is a situation where the medium within which signals travel degrade the signal. All networks experience this problem. The risk of attenuation depends on how you lay the cable. Take copper, for example. You should amplify the network by a switch or a hub after every 100 meters. If you use fiber optic, however, you get a longer distance before the network is degraded. Consider your organization needs, and if possible, use fiber optic cables instead of copper. However, if you cannot afford to use fiber optic cables, have a hub or switch in place accordingly to prevent attenuation.

- **Cross talk**

Wires that are in proximity to one another experience cross talk when they transmit current. To reduce the risk of cross talk, paired wires are twisted and set at 90 degrees from one another. The tighter you have the wires twisted, the less crosstalk you will experience on the network.

Chapter 4 Networking Macs and PCs

People often ask me about connecting Macs and PCs (IBM compatibles) together on the same network. Many have the mistaken idea that it cannot be done. In fact, it is not only possible, it is fairly simple to do as well.

So far, we've talked about two basic topologies for networking: LocalTalk and Ethernet. Both of these will also allow Macs and PCs to connect together on a network. LocalTalk can be used if you have a predominately Macintosh network and want to add some PCs to the network for specific purposes. Ethernet can be used for most anything including full PC networks with Macs and PCs sharing the resources. Ethernet works well for both Mac and PC networks and is a great medium for cross-platform applications.

What do you want to do?

The first thing to do when considering putting both types of computers on the same network is to decide what you really want to accomplish. Examples of goals for sharing a network might include:

Sharing files between Macs and PCs.

Sharing printers between Macs and PCs.

Having your Macintosh access a PC file server.

Using your Macintosh as a terminal on a mainframe or PC.

Providing a cross-platform E-mail solution.

Getting your PC to work more "like a Mac" on the network.

Getting your Mac to work like a PC on the network.

Each of these listed goals can be accomplished. Some are more simple than others, but all are possible and many have several possible solutions. For instance, sharing files is easily done when both systems can access the same file server. Printers can be shared when the PC has AppleTalk software installed or there is a Novell file server using Postscript printers on the network. A Macintosh can access many different types of file servers, can run a number of terminal applications, and can even access multiple mainframes simultaneously. E-mail solutions like QuickMail, Microsoft Mail, First Class, Eudora, and others offer client software for both Macs and PCs that make cross-platform communications even easier using file enclosures. We'll discuss in detail some of these options to get you started and to show how some of them can be accomplished. Just bear in mind that although Macs and PCs seem quite different (and are!), they are still computers and both speak the universal computer language of bits and bytes. That means that there is always a way to allow them to communicate — you just have to decide which way is best for you.

Macintosh Compatibility

There are several ways to be compatible on a network. But before we look at Macs **vs. PCs,** let's take a look at how Macs are compatible with PCs both on and off of networks. Macintosh computers are already compatible with PCs on three levels: file compatibility, PC emulation, and PC hardware compatibility.

File Compatibility

With file (or data) compatibility, Macintosh computers are able to read from and write to PC diskettes and read from PC CD ROMs. This means that a Macintosh user can take a diskette or CD from a PC user, insert it into his or her Macintosh, and read in a file from it. (This does NOT necessarily mean that a Mac can automatically run PC applications.) The Mac user can open the file, make changes, and (if it was on a diskette) write the changes back to the PC diskette. Much of this depends, of course, on having the right software running on your Macintosh. Usually, having the same program for each machine will do the trick. For instance, the

Mac user could be using Microsoft Word for Mac and the PC user using Microsoft Word for Windows.

This same level of compatibility can be accomplished over a network. If there is a common file storage area (like a Mac or Novell file server), both systems can access and make changes to files in that area. This is a very popular way to share information over a network.

PC Emulation

A Macintosh using PC emulation is actually "pretending" to be a PC through software. The most popular program to accomplish this is from Insignia Software and is called Soft PC or SoftWindows. Soft PC will emulate DOS on almost any Macintosh and will even emulate DOS networking through the network port on your Macintosh. SoftWindows 2.0 for the Power Macintosh will emulate a full 486 computer system running Windows 3.1 and is even reported to be compatible with Windows 95 as well.

These solutions are quite amazing to say the least, but do not offer the speed of a real 486 PC compatible system. However, for the Mac user who needs to occasionally access PC applications, they provide an excellent alternative to having two computers on his or her desk.

With SoftWindows on the Power Macintosh, you can emulate a full PC system in software including the Novell (or other type) network capabilities of a standard PC system. So, in effect, you can look just like a PC to the network. It can't tell the difference, so you can do almost anything with a Mac that a PC can do on a network.

PC Hardware Compatibility

In the last year or so, a new type of compatibility has been introduced into the arena by Apple. As of this writing, Apple makes two systems that include both a Macintosh computer and a PC-compatible (486DX2/ 66) computer in the same box. These systems allow the user to press a key combination to switch between the two systems. When you are on the Mac system, your keyboard, mouse, and monitor work as usual on your Macintosh. However, when you switch to the PC, your mouse, monitor, keyboard, even the network connection, CD ROM, disk drive, serial ports, and just about everything works on the PC. You are not emulating a PC system; you are actually running one.

With this level of hardware compatibility, you can now "have your cake and eat it, too," so to speak, by being able to run both systems in the space of **one.** This type system offers **a** great solution **to** anyone who **is a** Mac fan caught up in the midst of a PC office (or school), or anyone who needs **to** run a wide variety of software. With one of these systems, you can run just about anything you want to run. Whether it's PC or Macintosh-based, you can run it on this system. About all you need to do is switch to the correct side first, then install or run the software.

Of course, since this type system is a PC, you can attach it to a PC network and no one will be the wiser. You can even use the network for Mac networking as well.

In **1995,** Apple introduced **a** line of Power Macintosh systems with PCI slots. These will all provide similar hardware compatibility as an option. Apple and other vendors will be offering PC hardware solutions for these PCI machines. These cards should allow the new Macs to operate as PCs as well as Macintoshes. Already PCI cards are available with 80486 chips and cards, with Pentium processors should be just around the corner.

Using a PC on LocalTalk or PhoneNET

Although a PC on a Macintosh network is often considered to be the equivalent of an "enemy in the camp," it really isn't that hard to connect and use.

If you have a network made up of a number of Macintosh systems connected with LocalTalk or PhoneNET, there are a couple of options for you to add PCs to this network. There are still some manufacturers that produce an AppleTalk card for PCs. These cards plug into the "bus" of the PC and allow you to connect a LocalTalk or PhoneNET connector to them with a mini-DIN 8 connector, just like the printer port on **a** Macintosh. Farallon makes a card that includes the AppleTalk for PC software as well as Timbuktu Pro. With this card installed and a LocalTalk connector attached, a PC has many capabilities normally associated with a Macintosh on a network.

The LocalTalk connection allows the same basic features of an Ethernet network with the main exceptions of speed and some more advanced protocols. If you have the option, move up to Ethernet for best results.

Using a PC on a Macintosh Ethernet

If you want to set up a PC on your Macintosh Ethernet network, it is almost as easy. First of **all,** you'll need an Ethernet card for your **PC.** Be sure to get one that has the right kind of connector for your network (10Base-T, thinnet, etc.). The card will install in the bus slots and attach to the back of your PC. Be sure to run the setup software to install the correct drivers and to make sure the dip switches are set appropriately.

As you might imagine, this can be the most difficult part of connecting a PC to your network. PCs require settings to be made for all cards in the system to allow them to work on the computer. If you do not feel confident with this, or if you install a card and it doesn't work, don't waste a lot of time on it! Contact a consultant who knows what he/she is doing. It will save you a lot of time and effort and help you to get it right the first time.

The PC user can print to Postscript printers, mount Mac servers as additional hard drives on the computer, and even use Timbuktu to view and operate a Macintosh over the network. When a PC user mounts a Mac server, the server is assigned a drive letter (like E: or F:, etc.) and accessed just like any other PC hard drive.

Printers that are "chosen" by a PC using this software can be used by most PC applications by simply using the print command in the application. In some instances, you may have to do a special setup for the printer, but that is standard for most PC applications. With this Chooser software, you can even set it to automatically set up for printers and mount hard drives at startup and have them available to use each time you start the PC.

The Timbuktu connection actually allows you to either view a Mac screen from a PC or to view the PC (in Windows only) screen from a Macintosh. When viewing the PC from the Mac, you can control the mouse, keyboard, and monitor of the PC, doing pretty much all the same things a PC user can do. The opposite is also true. You can access the Macintosh from a PC and control the mouse, keyboard, and monitor of the Macintosh. This is great if you need to use a PC only occasionally. You can set up a PC on the network and make it available for Mac users to access when it is needed. *Note: Although Timbuktu can be used over LocalTalk, the speed of Ethernet will provide much better* results.

Another solution for file sharing for PCs and Macs is AppleShare 4.0.x from Apple. This program **is** packaged with **all** of the Apple Workgroup Servers and is also available separately if you already have a computer to use as a server. AppleShare has been around for quite a while and is very popular as a Macintosh network server. The current version allows not only Macs but PCs to be clients on the network. PCs using the AppleShare client software can share storage, printers, and even applications over the network with Macs.

A Macintosh on a PC Network

Using a PC on a Mac network means making it more of a Mac. However, using a Mac on a PC network is almost natural for the Macintosh. Of course, it will depend on what network software and hardware your PC network uses, but most server types have Macintosh client software available.

The most popular PC network software in use today is probably Netware, the server software from Novell. Novell Netware allows PCs to share storage areas and printers, load applications from the network and control access to certain areas of the server. Most popular PC applications are compatible with Novell Netware. Starting with Version 3.x and later, Novell software has included provisions for Macintosh computers to operate as clients on the network.

With Version 3.x, it was necessary to install a Macintosh NLM (Network Loading Module) on the server that would allow Macs to use the Novell server. Beginning with Version 4.0, the Mac server/client software was included with the server software. This software (or NLM) provides the instructions to allow the server to be compliant with the Apple FileSharing Protocol. This means that, to the Macintosh, the Novell server looks just like a

Macintosh server. You can go to Chooser, select AppleShare, and the Novell file server will be shown in the box to the right. Choose it and enter your name and password just like you do when you connect to an AppleShare File Server.

Connecting to WAN

Configuring a Serial Interface

Serial interfaces are typically used to interconnect client and ISP equipment.

Router(config)# interface serial 0/0/0

Moves to interface configuration mode.

Router(config-if)# ip address 7.7.7.7 255.255.255.248

Sets IPv4 address and network mask.

Router(config-if)# clock rate 64000

Sets interface clock rate to 64Kbit/s.

Router(config-if)# no shutdown

Enables interface.

Clock rate

If your device is DTE (client-side) you don't need to specify clock rate. Clock rate must be specified on DCE (service provider) equipment.

HDLC

For serial interface to work you need to specify encapsulation method, either HDLC or PPP. If you don't specify an encapsulation method then HDLC will be used.

Router(config)# interface serial 0/0/0

Moves to interface configuration mode.

Router(config-if)# encapsulation hdlc

Sets encapsulation to HDLC.

Encapsulation

HDLC encapsulation is already default setting on synchronous serial interfaces and you only need to use this command if you want to return to HDLC from another encapsulation method. Alternative encapsulation method for serial links is PPP.

PPP

PPP is an alternative to HDLC as an encapsulation method on serial links. You should use it when you are concerned about security. In other cases default HDLC works fine. This protocol has optional authentication capabilities – PAP (Password Authentication Protocol) and CHAP (Challenge Handshake Authentication Protocol).

#Configuring PPP encapsulation method:

Router(config)# interface serial 0/0/0

Moves to interface configuration mode.

Router(config-if)# encapsulation ppp

Sets encapsulation method to PPP.

Optional Tweaks:

Router(config-if)# ppp quality 90

Periodically checks PPP link for quality and sets quality threshold to 90%. If link quality goes below 90% link will shut down. This command is useful if you have a backup link available. This percentage threshold can be anything you prefer from 1 to 100.

Router(config-if)# compress mppc

Enables "mppc" compression algorithm. This reduces total traffic overhead on your serial link. Alternative compression algorithms for PPP are "predictor" and "stac".

#Configuring PAP (Password Authentication):

Step 1: Create a dummy user for authentication:

RouterOne(config)# username RouterTwo password PAP

Creates user "RouterTwo" with case-sensitive password set to "PAP". This is required to verify PAP authentication with peer.

Important: It's required that username equals hostname of the peering router and the password must be exactly the same for both dummy users.

RouterTwo(config)# username RouterOne password PAP

Creates user "RouterOne" with case-sensitive password set to "PAP".

Step 2: Configure serial interface for PAP authentication:

RouterOne(config)# interface serial 0/0/0

Moves to interface configuration mode.

RouterOne(config-if)# ppp authentication pap

Enables PAP authentication protocol.

RouterOne(config-if)# ppp pap sent-username RouterTwo password PAP

Sets user credentials for PAP authentication.

RouterTwo(config)# interface serial 0/0/0

Moves to interface configuration mode.

RouterTwo(config-if)# ppp authentication pap

Enables PAP authentication protocol.

RouterTwo(config-if)# ppp pap sent-username RouterOne password PAP

Sets user credentials for PAP authentication.

Note: Unfortunately PAP does not encrypt user credentials when exchanging authentication details. For security reasons it's recommended to use CHAP protocol instead.

#CHAP (Challenge Handshake Authentication):

Step 1: Create a dummy user for authentication.

RouterOne(config)# username RouterTwo password PAP

Creates user "RouterTwo" with case-sensitive password set to "PAP". This is required to verify PAP authentication with peer.

RouterTwo(config)# username RouterOne password PAP

Creates user "RouterOne" with case-sensitive password set to "PAP".

Step 2: Configure serial interface for CHAP authentication:

RouterOne(config)# interface serial 0/0/0

Moves to interface configuration mode.

RouterOne(config-if)# ppp authentication chap

Enables CHAP authentication protocol.

RouterTwo(config)# interface serial 0/0/0

Moves to interface configuration mode.

RouterTwo(config-if)# ppp authentication chap

Enables CHAP authentication protocol.

Frame Relay

Frame relay is a legacy technology that is mostly replaced by MPLS today. There are no more multipoint frame-relay clouds in modern service provider networks, but it's quite common to see it configured between a service provider and client devices.

#Configuring Frame Relay:

This example covers setting up PVC 100 and 101 on separate subinterfaces. Both subinterfaces are configured on the same s0/0/0 physical interface.

Router(config)# interface serial 0/0/0

Moves to interface configuration mode.

Router(config-if)# encapsulation frame-relay ietf

Sets frame relay encapsulation type to IETF. This also affects all the subinterfaces.

Router(config-if)# frame-relay lmi-type ansi

Sets LMI type to ANSI.

Router(config-if)# no shutdown

Enables interface.

Router(config-if)# exit

Moves back to global configuration mode.

Router(config)# interface serial 0/0/0.100 point-to-point

Creates a point-to-point subinterface .100 on s0/0/0 and moves to subinterface configuration mode.

Router(config-subif)# ip address 192.168.1.1 255.255.255.0

Sets IP address and network mask to the subinterface.

Router(config-subif)# frame-relay interface-dlci 100

Sets DLCI 100 to the subinterface.

#If you need to add another PVC just keep creating new subinterfaces:

Router(config)# interface serial 0/0/0.101 point-to-point

Creates a point-to-point subinterface .101 on s0/0/0 and moves to subinterface configuration mode.

Router(config-subif)# ip address 192.168.2.1 255.255.255.0

Sets IP address and network mask to the subinterface.

Router(config-subif)# frame-relay interface-dlci 101

Sets DLCI 101 to the subinterface.

#Show commands:

Router# show frame-relay pvc

Shows status of all PVCs configured.

Router# show frame-relay map

Shows DLCI map entries.

Router# show frame-relay lmi

Shows LMI stats.

Chapter 5 802. MAC fundamentals

Preamble 7 bytes	SOF 1 byte	Destination MAC address 6 bytes	Source MAC address 6 bytes	Length 2 bytes	Data / Pad 46 ... 1500 bytes		FCS 4 bytes

The IEEE 802.3 specifies the formats of frame or structures of the frame. The fundamental format of the frame needs adjustments to align with the individual needs of the transmission system. The update of the given Ethernet variant will contain the adjustments needed to the Ethernet frame.

Ethernet MAC data frame format of 10/100 Mbps

The 802.3 is the basic MAC data frame format used within the 10/100 Mbps systems. The fundamental frame consists of seven elements that prioritize the following areas:

Start of frame delimiter: It consists of 1 byte as well as alternating series of 1s and 0s and must terminate with two 1s.

The destination address: It is a field that contains the node's address for which the data is required. A 1 denotes a group address while a 0 denotes an individual address. The subsequent bit into the destination address segment to determine local and global addresses. If the address is administered in a global way, then the bit will be one and zero if it is administered locally. The 46 bits which are still unused are used for the destination address itself.

Source address: It compromises of 6 bytes, and it denotes the sending station. In line with all individual addresses, the leftmost bit will always be a zero.

Length or type: It is a field of 2 bytes in size. The field has MAC details and shows the client data types of the client all of which are included in the information section of the frame. The length field sometimes indicates the ID of the frame which is made by the help of a format that is optional.

- *Payload*

The data block has the payload information. Most of the time, it is about 1500 bytes long. In an instance where the length of the field is below 46 bytes, then the data used for padding are integrated to make the length up to the needed minimum of forty-six bytes.

- *Trailer*

The check sequence of the frame which is abbreviated as FCS is a field that is four bytes long and is made up of a 32-bit redundancy check that is cyclic, CRC, that is generated on the address of the destination, address of the source, and length and data sections.

Ethernet Mac data frame format for 1000 Mbps

When it comes to 802.3z systems, the fundamental frame of data of MAC format for Ethernet is modified slightly. A frame can be modified to enable it to fit the minimum and maximum specifications.

Half-duplex transmission

The half-duplex transmission entails the use of carrier sense multiple access/collision detection, and it was designed to allow multiple nodes to exchange on common media without the requiring switching, assigned timeslots, and controllers. In this setup, each node can determine when it should transmit, and the network is self-organizing. The carrier sense multiple collision or access detection protocols are applied for Ethernet.

Collision detects: The nodes on a network may sometimes find a passive network, but two nodes may virtually start transmitting at the same time. In such a scenario, the data exchange will collide. With collision detect, the two nodes can sense and halt data exchange on the connection or network. The computer network nodes will then temporarily stop transmission and wait for a random time slice before making another attempt to send the data on the connection or network. The role of this random wait is to avoid two nodes from again starting to exchange data on the connection or network at virtually the same time.

Full duplex

Equally important, the MAC of the Ethernet allows for the full-duplex exchange of data implying that data is simultaneously sent in both directions of communicating nodes on a computer network. However, full-duplex exchange of data occurs on node-to-node connections and is easier to function about the CSMA/CD approach. The speeds of full-duplex exchange of data are higher compared to CSMA/CD when the network is being utilized. The full duplex transmission also eliminates the need to time sending of data as they are only two nodes on the connection or network connection.

Ethernet addresses

A MAC address refers to a distinct identifier given to each network interface card in an Ethernet. The maker of the network circuit gives the unique identifier, and the maker satisfies the stipulated IEEE guidelines for obtaining and assigning the unique identifier to the network interface card. The unique MAC address consists of a number with 48 bits where the initial 24-bits show who the maker is and is known as the ID of the creator or sometimes the Unique Identifier of the organization that is given by the authority that does registrations. The producer gives the remaining portion of the address, and it is referred to as the augmentation of the board ID. Usually, the MAC address is programmed into the hardware implying that it can't be modified and since the MAC address is allocated to the NIC, it remains unchanged on the computer. For this reason, it is possible to remotely communicate with the user since the MAC address is unique.

The figure below shows the MAC architecture:

Issues of MAC

Wireless communication does not have any physical boundary, unlike the wired or Ethernet connection. For wired communication, the sender is certain that data transmitted at one end will reach the other end because of the well-defined physical boundary of wire. As a result, the idea of acknowledging per frame arose to ensure the same level of reliability in 802.11. Using this approach, the receiver will send an acknowledge status of each frame received. The sender becomes sure concerning the delivery of a packet after receiving an ack from the receiver end sender. Should the ack be absent, then there is a possibility that the receiver did not receive the frame or the frame could have been corrupted during transmission. When such happens, the sender will resend the frame.

Exercise

a. What are some of the issues with MAC concerning frames transmission?

Chapter 6 802.11 Framing

There are three 802.11 kinds of the frame that have several subcategory frames. These types of frame are data frames, control frames, and management frames.

Management Frames

Many frames in a wireless LAN are management frames for 802.11 standards. These frames are utilized with wireless nodes to leave and join the set assigned for primary services. The other name for management frames for 802.11 standards is the media access control protocol unit of data. The information elements are of variable lengths in management frames.

There are several subcategories of the management frame and these are:

Association response

- Action no ACK
- Timing advertisement
- Re-association request
- Association request
- Probe response
- Disassociation
- Re-association response
- Authentication
- Announcement of traffic indication notification

- Beacon
- Action
- Probe request
- De-authentication

Control Frames

The delivery of the frames of data is realized through 802.11 control frames. The control frames are transmitted at one of the fundamental rates. Equally important is that control frames are essential in acquiring the channel, clear the channel, and offer unicast frame confirmations, and they have data about the header.

There are several subcategories of the control frame:

- Request to send
- Power save poll
- Clear to send
- Contention free-end
- Acknowledgment
- Block ACK request
- CF-End+ CF-ACK
- Control wrapper
- Block ACK
- Data Frames

Frames of data can be considered as the units of transmission on a network that contain adequate information for devices to acknowledge, direct, drop, merge, or extend data being transmitted. Through frames, it becomes possible to add encryption and other adjustments to the individual packet. The layers 3 to layer seven service data unit payloads are encrypted for data privacy reasons. A higher retry manifesting with the high counter score when analyzing packets on a network indicates noise, and eventually, the network will have slow connections as well as overall low quality of service.

There are fifteen subcategories of data frames, and these are:

- **Null function**
- **QoS CF-Poll**
- **Data**
- **Data+CF-poll**
- **CF-poll**
- **Data+CF-ACK**
- **Data+CF-ACK+CF-Poll**
- **QoS Data**
- **QoS Data+CF-ACK+CF-Poll**
- **CF-ACK**
- **QoS Null**
- **QoS Data+CF-Poll**
- **QoS Data+ CF-ACK**
- **QoS CF-ACK+CF-Poll**

Beacon management frame

These are the core aspects of the wireless connection or network. The access point of a fundamental service set transmits the beacons while the nodes listen for the frames of the beacon. The client nodes only send beacons when taking part in an independent fundamental service which is also known as Ad Hoc mode. Client nodes use a timestamp present in each beacon to maintain their clocks synchronized with the access points. Since most of the successful wireless communication builds on timing, it is critical that all stations be in synchronization with each other. The frame of the beacon has all the critical information for a node to understand the fundamental service variables before joining the fundamental service set. The transmission rate of beacons is around ten times per second. On some access points, the interval can be modified, but it can't be deactivated.

Exercise

    a. Why is beacon service the most critical service in wired LANs?

    b. Why is it important for smart network devices to augment frames to satisfy the minimum length before transmission? Think of having the networking devices having to frequently drop frames until they encounter a frame that satisfies the specified length before transmission.

    c. Encryption is critical in network transmission to ensure privacy. Encryption is considered as the last resort in security as it simply implies that should a malicious attacker intercept data, then the data will be jumbled up and will not make sense to the attacker assuming that the attacker cannot decrypt the data. It is important to ensure that encryption remains transparent in a wireless LAN. Justify why encryption and decryption should remain transparent.

Chapter 7 Unified Communications and Virtualization

Unified communications refers to the process of integrating real-time services such as instant messaging, services, presence, VoIP, and video/audioconferencing using non-real-time services of communication such as voicemail and email. Devices for unified communications include the use of specialized devices, servers, and gateways.

At the lowest level, the unified communications merges the data and telephone networks. There are several vendors who provide us with services, applications and equipment for unified communications. Examples of these include Microsoft, HP, Dell, NEC, and IBM. The following are some of the unified communications products from Cisco:

- Cisco Unified Communications Manager IM and Presence

- Cisco Unified Communications Manager Express (CME)

- Cisco Unity Connection (Unity)

- Cisco Unified Communications Manager (CUCM)

The CME is used as the call agent in organizations which are small. After integration of this with the default gateway router, the CME can virtually control what happens on a device such as an IP phone. Consider the devices which have been laid out as shown below:

Once the user uses the IP phone, an off-hook state will have to be sent from IP phone to the SME router by use of either SIP or Skinny Client Control protocol (SCCP). Once the user is through with dialing of the phone, the call will be forwarded by the CME router to the PSTN connected interface. At this point, the CME router will be assuming the role of a voice gateway, and a signal will be send to the PSTN so as to establish a call on the place of the IP Phone, a Cisco one. The CME router will have established two connections of the call. One will be for the IP phone, while the other one will be for PSTN.

The functionalities of CUCM are similar to those of CME, but it was developed for larger organizations. CUCM has the following features:

- **It fully supports audio and video telephony.**
- Offers an appliance-based operation which always runs on top of a secure and hardened operating system.
- VMware installation which is to be deployed in virtual machines.
- Redundant server cluster which can scale up to 40,000 phones.
- Disaster Recovery System (DRS) which is built-in and which can allow for database backup in a secured FTP server.

- Directory service support with the capability of incorporating user accounts.

The Cisco Unity Connection is aimed at making messages retrievable from any device which is voice-enabled or an application. The message can be retrieved by use of many clients, regardless of the state in which it was left. The Cisco Unity Connection has the following features:

- 20,000 mailboxes for each server.
- Access voicemails which can be accessed from anywhere.
- Directory server integration.
- Microsoft Exchange support.

The Cisco Unity Connections functions independently of the CUCM, and it has not been exclusively tied to the CUCM product. This means that the connection has to be set like an outside system which can be able to communicate with the CUCM by use of SIP or SCCP.

Quality of Service

Unified Communications strongly rely on Quality of service policies. Real-time video and audio streams of data are very sensitive to the issues to do with quality. Let us discuss some of these issues:

- Delay- this is the time that a packet requires to travel from its source to the destination.

- Jitter- this is a variable delay, or uneven arrival of packets.
- Drops- packet drops will occur when a link has become congested and the interface queue of the router has overflowed.

Switches and routers can be configured with features of QoS so as to mitigate the issues by prioritization and classification of traffic. The following are the three ways that we can implement QoS:

- Best-effort- this is similar to no QoS, and it utilizes the FIFO (first in first out) queuing strategy. This means that the emptying of the packets from the queue is done in the same order in which they arrived.
- Integrated Service (IntServ)- this makes use of strict bandwidth reservations and that is why it is referred to as hard QoS. However, it lacks scalability, since it has to be configured for every router along the path of the packet.
- Differentiated Services (DiffServ)- each packet has been marked, and the routers and switches have to use these markings when forwarding these packets. It is always referred to as a soft QoS, since it does not make any explicit reservation. Most modern configurations of the QoS are based on this approach.

The following QoS mechanisms are used when treating packets by use of the DiffServ mechanism:

1. Classification- the traffic has to be placed in different categories without the altering of bits.
2. Marking- the altering of bits is done within the frames, or packet, or cell and this indicates how the packet should treated by the network.
3. Congestion avoidance- package drops occur when a queue has filled to capacity, and for this to be avoided, we can configure the minimum threshold for the purpose of random early detection (RED). After detection of this, packets whose priority is low can be discarded. This can be done until the maximum has been reached, and the low-priority packets will have been dropped.
4. Policing and shaping- instead of having to make a minimum amount of bandwidth which is available for traffic of certain types, some people are in need of limiting the bandwidth which is available. With traffic-shaping and policing tools, you can easily achieve this.
5. Link efficiency- if you need to make your limited bandwidth available to the links with slower-speed, you can decide to implement either interleaving, link fragmentation, or compression.

Virtualization

Platforms for unified communications are often virtualized, especially in implementations which are large. Network, device, and data virtualizations are the trends which will continue to impact how computer networks are designed and implemented.

Server Virtualizations

A single high-end server has enough computing power for handling the tasks from multiple independent servers. In data centers, the server hardware has been specialized to provide a flexible and efficient platform so as to meet the customers' needs.

Networking Device Virtualization

The virtualization feature has also been implemented in the networking field, since it is possible for one to virtualize devices such as firewalls, switches, and routers. For you to establish a connection between the virtual work and the physical world, you have to do it through a physical interface which will connect to the virtual interfaces. It is possible for you to configure more than one virtual interface to use one physical interface.

The use of virtual interfaces enables network administrators to apply same QoS and security policies which would have been used on the physical networking devices.

Software-Defined Networking

Without the use of orchestration software, it would have been difficult for us to manage large implementations of networking devices and virtualized servers. Software-defined networking is aimed at managing this type of complexity, and making it to be relatively simple for networkers. With SDN solutions, the administrator can implement functions, features, and configurations without having to do the configuration of the individual networking devices on the command line. This can only be achieved by separation of the data plane from the physical network control plane. It is also possible for the control plane to manage several devices.

Cloud Concepts

Virtualization forms the foundation for cloud computing. The services model for the cloud computing includes the following:

1. Software as a Service (SaaS)- the cloud service provider is tasked with accessing services such as emails, virtual desktops, and communications which have been delivered over the Internet.

2. Platform as a service (PaaS)- the cloud service provider is tasked with accessing the development services and tools which are used for delivering the applications.

3. Infrastructure as a Service- the cloud service provider is tasked with accessing the virtualized network services, network equipment, and supporting the network infrastructure.

The National Institute of Standards and Technology (NIST) has also defined 4 delivery models which include the following:

1. Private cloud- this is created for use in a single organization. The organization may own this, or it may

be owned by a third party such as a cloud service provider.

2. Public cloud- this is created so that it can be used by the general public. The physical location of the infrastructure is on the site of the cloud service provider, but one or multiple organizations may own it.

3. Community cloud- this is created for some named organizations of the same type in that they share some concerns.

4. Hybrid cloud- this is made up of two or more clouds which bear several distinct types. These can be community, public, or private.

Storage Area Networks

Data which the virtualization and cloud services have made available is physically located in the storage area networks (SANs). A SAN is just a network which has storage devices with the capability of making the storage devices appear as if they have been attached locally.

Directly Attached Storage

The implementation of this is shown below:

In this type of connection, each server is directly connected to its own hard drive, and this can be an internal or external hard drive. This connection is implemented using a Small Computer System Interface (SCSI), and this is simply a collection of standards which can be used for the exchange of data between computers and the storage devices. The users will have to use Ethernet so as to establish connections to the servers.

Network-Attached Storage

In this type of connection, a storage resource can be used by more than one server.

Fibre Channel

In this type of connection, access to the storage area is done by a fiber channel (FC) at a very high speed. The implementation is very popular in SANs which are enterprise-level. Servers connecting to an FC network should have two different adapters, that is, a host bus adapter for connecting the SAN and a standard NIC adapter for connecting the LAN. The HBA card will allow the server to establish a connection to the FC network.

Fibre Channel over Ethernet

This is a new evolution of fiber networks, and in this case, the servers only need one adapter so as to establish a connection to the network. The technology allows FC frames to be wrapped inside the Ethernet frames and then be sent over the Ethernet LAN, and these can run up to a speed of 10Gbps. The data transport in this case is Ethernet until our traffic has reached the FCoE switch. The FC data transport is then applied to the FC SAN. iSCSI

FCoE SANs and the FC SANs though modern can be too expensive for implementations ranging from small and medium. With the iSCSI implementation of the network, it will be possible for us to sent the SCSI commands inside the IP packets, meaning that we will be in a position to remotely access a SAN over an IP network. Compared to an FCoE implementation, the performance of an iSCSI is a bit lower, but it is liked for implementation due to its low cost.

Chapter 8 Future protocols

The wide areas of applications of wireless networks in modern times are an indication of what the technology will offer in the future. At the moment, wireless networks have simplified a lot of human activities such as communication, business transactions, and other activities. However, the future is brighter than most people can imagine. The modern wireless network will be child's play compared to what the future promises. Let's consider some of the major future development of wireless networks and the potential huge impact they will have on the users. Let me start with Li-Fi.

Li-Fi

You obviously are aware of the attributes and usefulness of the Wi-Fi wireless technology. As a reminder, this technology is one of the best things that has ever happened to wireless technology. Wi-Fi has really simplified wireless connection and makes it accessible to millions of users around the world. However, a better version of this wireless network is around the corner. Welcome to the world of Li-Fi. What is Li-Fi?

Li-Fi, Light Fidelity, is the new poster boy of wireless communication technology. This technology carries out data communication through light signals. One of the biggest advantages of this technology is its impressive speed. At the moment, this wireless technology can boast of a speed of 224 gigabits/second. When compared with its predecessor, Wi-Fi, this is a good improvement with tons of benefits for wireless connection users. Professor Harald Hass introduced Li-Fi into the world at a TED Talk in 2011. He had the dream of turning the light bulbs into a better use: wireless routers. Today, he is working towards achieving that dream and may do so in the near future.

To work on his dream, Professor Hass launched Pure Li-Fi after the Talk in 2012. The company was established as a platform for developing Li-Fi product. The company is primarily responsible for developing Li-Fi devices. During the Talk, Professor Hass unveiled his dream.

Since the professor has successfully proved that the light spectrum can be a good medium of data transmission, Li-Fi is then considered as an optical wireless communication medium. Li-Fi communicates data through ultra-violet (visible light) and infra-red waves. The two spectrums have the ability to carry more information than its radio frequency waves counterpart, which explains why Li-Fi is faster than Wi-Fi.

Currently, this technology depends on the light from light-emitting diodes (LEDs) for data communication. Of course, LEDs have a reputation for their low environmental impact, efficiency, and longevity. When this project sees the light of day, you can turn the lights in your office or home into wireless routers. Since LED light bulbs fall into the semiconductor group, the constant electricity the bulb receives can be altered to be dimmer or brighter, depending on your choice.

With the assistance of Visible Light Communication, the current received by the LED bulb can be flicked on and off at an extremely high rate. If you want to access the Li-Fi network, you need a component that can be used for deciphering the light signals as well as a device for light signal detection.

How does it work?

The Li-Fi network works on a very simple principle. First, a LED light bulb is fed with data and subsequently has a signal processing technology interfaced. The data is pulsed by the LED bulb at a high rate to the photodetector. When the photodetector receives the pulses, it interprets the pulse into an electrical signal. The signal is subsequently converted into binary data, the web content we all use.

Thus, the LED lights are later networked to make data accessible to multiple users through a single LED light or shift from a LED light to another while their access remains unaffected by the move. Li-Fi's high speed and spatial limits can be combined with Wi-Fi and cellular technologies as a connectivity option. The technology is very useful for siphoning off heavy traffic from Wi-Fi and cellular networks. For instance, this technology can be made available in sports stadiums, shopping malls, and other densely populated areas to allow users to consume live streaming, videos, and other content-rich media. When people are using Li-Fi, the capacities of Wi-Fi and cellular networks in the area will be freed up. Naturally, uplinks don't use much capacity like the downlinks with its network-straining capability.

One of the biggest challenges that experts are facing about the Internet of Things (IoT) revolution is how to find the huge capacity needed to handle the data. Well, Li-Fi has come to the rescue. It has proven to be an efficient, viable, and secure solution to that problem. An office, a home, or a factory can leverage the power of the Li-Fi technology for running its high capacity network while the public capacity is not affected in any way.

Car-to-Car Communication

In the future, a simple wireless technology will take over driving challenges and make our roads safer with reduced accidents. The technology is designed to warn drivers of impending collisions to enable them to prepare in advance to prevent the collision. Known as vehicle-to-vehicle or car-to-car communication, the technology will let cars on the road broadcast their speed, position, brake status, steering-wheel position, and other relevant information to other road users within a couple of meters of the car.

This valuable information will be used by the other cars to have a general view of what is going on around them and notify them of potential troubles that even the most cautious and experienced driver may miss. By building anticipation for the potential collision, the driver is best poised to take all necessary precautions to avoid the accident.

At the moment, many cars are equipped with ultrasound or radar technology for detecting vehicles or obstacles. Despite the usefulness of these technologies, their limited sensor range is a big issue to contend with. Cars equipped with the technology can see beyond the nearest obstruction, making it pale in comparison with the car-to-car wireless technology that will soon take over in the nearest future. With over five million accidents recorded in the United States alone every year, resulting in over 30,000 fatal cases, this technology will be a welcome development. At the moment, Japan and Europe are already testing this technology. It is a matter of time before other countries embrace this amazing wireless and life-saving technology.

The Internet of Things

When people hear the term, Internet of Things, different ideas are formed. Thus, the concept is shrouded in confusion and mystery as it means different things to people from different walks of life.

IoT also comprises micro-electromechanical (MEMS) systems. When MEMS are embedded into an object, it allows you to communicate and interact effectively with the environment. The objects that can be used include controllers in oil refineries and humans with implanted medical devices. Thus, regardless of the numerous definitions of the concept, it is estimated that tens of billions of devices will enjoy Internet connection by 2020. To realize this vision, much is dependent on wireless technology. What happens to the connected billions of devices?

The connected devices have the capacity to generate information and data that Internet users from all walks of life can access regardless of their places of residence. Therefore, businesses, governments, and individuals are allowed to use the information for making real-time data-driven decisions. In the future, the IoT has tons of areas of applications that will be explored as the technology fully matures. Let's take a look into some of the practical uses of this wireless technology in the future.

More cities will become smart

At the moment, the IoT wireless technology is embraced mostly by homeowners. This trend is expected to continue in the future, although more cities are expected to adopt this technology. Then, companies and cities will turn to the wireless technology to save time and money in addition to becoming more efficient. The adoption of the technology means that cities can be automated and remotely managed. Useful data can also be collected through video camera surveillance systems, visitor kiosks, taxis, and even bike rental stations.

Artificial intelligent will become the real "thing"

Thermostats, home hubs, lighting systems, and others will collect data on your pattern of usage and habits. The voice-controlled devices in your home will record whatever you tell them and store the recordings in the cloud. The data collection has a goal: facilitate machine learning.

Machine learning is an integral part of artificial learning because it is designed to help computers "learn" without being programmed for specific uses. The computers are designed to pay attention to whatever information they collect and use the information to learn. In the future, the machines can really learn your preferences through series of data collection and adjust themselves to meet your preferences.

Routers will become more "smarter" and secure

Routers are mostly used in homes and are vulnerable to attacks because users can't install security software on them. The craze for the adoption of IoT in the consumer market has placed the necessity on manufacturers to make their products available in the market as soon as possible. The impact is that sometimes these manufacturers pay little or no attention to security in their bid to hit the market before their competitors. The home router becomes handy here.

As previously discussed, the router serves as the Internet's entry point into your home. It is true that the connected devices have no way of self-protection, but the router can provide entry point protection. Although the current routers provide some protection through firewalls, password protection, and the ability to be configured to grant access to some selected devices, they are still prone to attacks because they don't have security software installed on them. Thus, malware can still find a way around the security measures and gain access to a network.

82

Currently, attackers are focusing on effective ways they can exploit the vulnerabilities in IoT devices. In the future, routers will come fully equipped with built-in security software programs that are more effective at shutting off potential intruders than what the current security measure can offer.

Wearables will remain a niche

It is estimated that by the end of 2018, over 12 million wearables will be sold in the US alone due to the increased adoption of Google Assistant and Amazon Alexa in more devices. The hype surrounding these devices has provided marketers with a new way of dealing with customers. It is expected that the manufacturers and marketers of these devices will not rest on their oars but will build more of these wearables in the future to meet the growing needs for these efficient wireless technologies that have wormed their ways into the hearts of millions of users from all walks of life.

Cloud computing

Cloud computing offers some benefits that make it a very important technology both now and in the future. A couple of its numerous benefits are:

- *Cost effective:* With cloud computing, you have to think less about buying software and hardware, a very expensive thing. You also don't have to bother yourself with setting up and running datacenters and spending a huge sum of money on round-the-clock electricity, racks of servers, and IT experts that will manage the infrastructure. This saves you a huge amount of money.

- *Speed:* Speed is another benefit you can enjoy from using cloud computing. Whatever computing resources you need will be delivered to you within a couple of minutes. You only need a few mouse clicks to access the services. This will give your business the desired flexibility while the pressure of capacity planning will be taken off you.

- *Performance:* A global network of datacenters is used for running cloud computing services; these datacenters are upgraded regularly by using the latest computing hardware that offers speed and efficiency. Thus, you have access to better resources rather than what a single corporate datacenter can ever offer you. It also offers greater economies of scale and reduced network latency.

- *Reliability:* Disaster recovery, data backup, and other related services are less expensive and easier through data computing. This is because the technology allows data to be mirrored.

Many people, including inventors and technology enthusiasts, are optimistic about the future of wireless technology. The availability of the needed resources and the increasing demand for more wireless devices ensure that inventors will still feed humanity with more technologies that will make life easier and better in the future.

Chapter 9 Switching

Modern switches are extremely robust with layer 3 models performing functions originally reserved for routers such as running routing protocols. They are used from the access layer to the core of the network, and in some designs even on the edge. You will certainly be configuring many switches and should have a very strong knowledge of their basics.

Creating/Verifying VLANs

Managed switches are capable of creating multiple Virtual LANs or VLANS on a single physical switch. This allows for Layer 2 separation between different ports on the same switch, logically similar to multiple physical switches.

Between multiple VLANs, the only way to have these separate subnets communicate is through the use of a Layer 3 device performing routing. The Layer 3 switch itself could serve this function, as we'll see later!

To assign ports to different vlans, the VLAN must first be created. To create a vlan, use the (config)# vlan command to enter VLAN configuration mode. Specify a vlan number between 1 and 4094. In general it is best to use vlans 1-1001 due to limitations with extended vlans, although VLAN 1006-4094 are available if needed.

If you were wondering, vlans 1002-1005 are reserved for bridging legacy L2 technologies to Ethernet, such as token ring and fddi, and cannot be configured or disabled by users.

To create a vlan, simply enter (config)# vlan **vlan_number**. The name command assigns a name to the vlan, much like the "description" command for interfaces.

(config)# vlan 501

(config-vlan)# name "User Network"

To verify the vlans configured on the device, use the #show vlan command.

#show vlan

The output of the #show vlan command lists the vlan numbers, names, and ports assigned to each vlan.

Configuring Switch Ports

To configure switch ports, enter interface configuration mode via the global configuration mode command (config)# interface **port_type port_number**

Examples of port types are FastEthernet, GigabitEthernet, and Serial.

The port number is usually represented by two or three numbers separated by forward slashes. For example gigabitEthernet 0/1 or gigabitEthernet 1/0/1. Typically the first number is the switch number, the second is the module number on that switch, and the last is the port number on that module. This varies on different hardware platforms.

To modify the configuration of the first port on a 3750X-24P Switch, execute the following commands:

Switch(config)#interface gigabitEthernet 1/0/1

Switch(config-if)#description "User Port"

Switch(config-if)#switchport access vlan 501

Switch(config-if)#switchport mode access

Switchport access vlan 501 assigns the port to vlan 501, and switchport mode access designates the port as an access, or user facing, port - which is the default setting.

Multiple interfaces can likewise be configured simultaneously using the interface range command, this case ports 1-24 on switch 1.

Switch(config)#interface range gigabitEthernet 1/0/1-24

Switch(config-if)#description "User Port"

Switch(config-if)#switchport access vlan 501

Switch(config-if)#switchport mode access

Configuring Routed Interfaces

Sometimes it's necessary to turn a port on a switch to a layer 3 routing interface. This allows the interface to be assigned an IP address directly, behaving just like an interface on a router. Simply specify the (config-if)#no switchport command on the interface to enable this mode.

Switch(config)#interface GigabitEthernet1/0/2

Switch(config-if)#description "Routed Port"

Switch(config-if)#no switchport

Switch(config-if)#ip address 10.10.10.10 255.255.255.0

Configuring Switch Vlan Interfaces (SVIs)

It is possible to create a layer 3 interface on a vlan. This interface can be used for management, for running a DHCP server, or for serving as a default gateway for a subnet. This type of virtual interface is called a Switch VLAN interface or SVI. It is configured very similarly to a physical interface. This IP address can be reached from any port on the associated VLAN.

TIP

Traffic between SVIs is routed by default if ip routing is enabled - meaning two VLANs with SVIs can communicate, even if that was not intended!

Switch(config)#interface Vlan501

Switch(config-if)#description "User SVI"

Switch(config-if)#ip address 10.127.0.1 255.255.255.128

Notice from the #show interface vlan 501 command that the SVI behaves just like a normal physical interface.

Enabling IP Routing

To use SVIs or routed interfaces to perform routing functions on Layer 3 switches ip routing must be enabled using the following command:

(config)#ip routing

This allows a Layer 3 switch to forward traffic just like a router.

Configuring Trunk Ports

Trunk ports can transport data from multiple vlans through tagging packets with VLAN information. Some uses include connecting multiple switches together allowing the same vlans to be accessed across multiple switches, for wireless access points which need to broadcast SSIDs for multiple VLANs, or for virtual hosts whose VMs need access to multiple VLANs.

To create a trunk port the switch port must be configured in trunk mode and the encapsulation type must be specified. In this case we will be using IEEE 802.1Q, an open standard.

The native vlan is used for all untagged traffic, meaning if the switch receives a packet with no tagging it is assigned to the native vlan. The allowed vlan command allows only the specified VLANs to traverse the trunk. Industry wide practice is to explicitly specify the vlans which are allowed to prevent unauthorized traffic to travel across the trunk.

Switch(config)#int range gi 1/0/22-24

Switch(config-if-range)#description "Wireless AP Trunk"

Switch(config-if-range)#switchport trunk encapsulation dot1q

Switch(config-if-range)#switchport trunk native vlan 502

Switch(config-if-range)#switchport   trunk   allowed   vlan
501,502,503,505

Switch(config-if-range)#switchport mode trunk

Voice Vlans

If you are using Cisco IP Phones, it is possible to create special trunk ports which allow a single ethernet cable to pass a data VLAN for clients and a Voice VLAN for phones. This is meant for access ports connected to Cisco phones.

To enable this feature, use the (config-if)#switchport voice vlan command on the interface. Notice in the configuration below one port is a member of two vlans without "being in trunk mode".

(config)# int gi 1/0/1

(config-if)# switchport access vlan 20

(config-if)# switchport mode access

(config-if)# switchport voice vlan 40

Power Over Ethernet (POE)

POE allows powering devices using ethernet cabling while still transmitting data. This technology is very useful for many applications, such as wireless access points (WAPs), security cameras, and VOIP phones. It can be very difficult and costly to run dedicated power to every device and POE allows a method to only run one cable instead of two.

There are two major POE standards, 802.3af and 802.3at sometimes known as POE+. The major difference between them is the maximum power delivered, at 15 Watts and 30 Watts, respectively.

To configure POE on switch ports, use the (config-if)#power inline command. By default, POE switch ports are set to autonegotiate power requirements with POE devices. If you would like to manually disable POE on a switch port, use the following command.

(config)# interface gi 0/1

(config-if)# power inline never

And to re enable it again:

(config)# interface gi 0/1

(config-if)# power inline auto

To view the status of POE on the switch, you can use the #show power inline command, which shows information such as the total and currently used power, as well as the POE devices connected to which port and their power draw. In the example below, you can see 3 generic POE devices using 4 Watts each, and a Cisco IP Phone 7961 using 6.3 Watts.

Spanning Tree Protocol (STP)

Spanning Tree Protocol is used to prevent layer 2 loops from forming between meshed switches. Loops are very dangerous as they are capable of bringing down an entire network by saturating links or overloading the CPU of switches. STP prevents loops by disabling redundant links, making sure there is only one path is active at any time. STP is enabled by default on Cisco switches, helping to protect against loops.

In the example below the redundant link to Switch 3 from Switch 2 is disabled via STP, preventing Layer 2 loops.

It is good practice to manually select which switch will be the root, as this switch will be doing the STP calculations for the entire network. The most powerful switch on the network, such as the core switches, would make prime candidates. If you do not select which switch will become root, the slowest, oldest switch on your network could be elected root!

The STP root is elected by having the lowest bridge priority, and in the case of a tie, having the lowest mac address. To configure the spanning tree root primary and secondary, use the following commands:

(config)#spanning-tree vlan 1-4094 root primary

(config)#spanning-tree vlan 1-4094 root secondary

The above commands change the priority from default (32768) to 24576 (primary) and 28672 (secondary).

There are several STP protocols, with STP being the oldest. Other STP protocols include MST (Multiple Spanning Tree) and RPVST (Rapid Per-VLAN Spanning Tree). It is a good idea to enable RPVST on your switches, as it can greatly decrease convergence time from 30-60 seconds which are typical in STP.

(config)#spanning-tree mode rapid-pvst

Spanning tree functions by disabling a port while some time to test for loops when a device is first plugged in. This can be very annoying for your clients, as it may take 30-60 seconds to get a link after plugging into the network! A typical solution to this problem is by bypassing the STP check for access ports. This can be enabled with the portfast feature on the interface:

(config)#interface gio/5

(config-if)#spanning-tree portfast

Cisco IOS warns you that using portfast can cause bridging loops. To help mitigate this issue, BPDU Guard can be used. BPDU guard checks a port for Bridge Protocol Data Units (BPDU), which are special packets used by spanning-tree. If one is detected, the port is disabled, and it will need to be manually re enabled later. This ensures no loops can be formed in the network.

To configure BPDU guard, use the command below:

(config-if)#spanning-tree bpduguard enable

Verifying Spanning Tree

The #show spanning tree command shows information about the STP root, the switch's STP configuration, and the STP status of the interfaces on the switch.

#show spanning-tree

The #show spanning-tree summary command shows a brief overview of the STP status, such as the STP mode used, and the number of ports on each vlan in each STP state.

Vlan Trunking Protocol (VTP)

VLAN Trunking Protocol is a protocol developed to simplify the management of VLANs among multiple switches. A switch can be configured as a VTP server which allows all VTP clients to receive VLAN information automatically so it is not necessary to manually create VLANs on each switch.

All switches managed by VTP must be in the same VTP domain, they must be given a role (master, server, transparent, or off) and they can optionally be configured with a password.

S1(config)#vtp domain mydomain

S1(config)#vtp mode server

S1(config)#vtp password mypassword

S2(config)#vtp domain mydomain

S2(config)#vtp mode client

S2(config)#vtp password mypassword

TIP

Don't forget to configure trunk ports between the switches so they can pass vlan information via VTP.

S1(config)# interface gi 0/1

S1(config-if)#switchport trunk encapsulation dot1q

S1(config-if)#switchport mode trunk

S2(config)# interface gi 0/1

S2(config-if)#switchport trunk encapsulation dot1q

S2(config-if)#switchport mode trunk

Verifying VTP

The #show vtp status command gives an overview of the VTP process, including VTP version number, VTP mode, and VTP domain.

After creating vlan 66 and 77 on S1, the same VLANs show up automatically on S2! Check with the #show vlan command.

Link Aggregation (LAG)

Link Aggregation is used to combine multiple physical interfaces into one logical interface, increasing bandwidth and providing redundancy should one link fail. Because all ports are logically combined, redundant links within a LAG are not disabled via STP.

LAG is typically used to connect switches together on the backbone or for connecting high bandwidth servers such as virtual hosts or file servers to your network.

With LAG up to eight ports can be configured as one aggregated port. However, if we combine two 1gb ports we have an overall bandwidth of 2 gbps but the max throughput for any session is still just 1 gbps.

Why? Only one logical session can pass over a single link at any time. For example, Computer A can speak to Computer B using one of the aggregated links and at the same time Computer C can speak to Computer D on the other. One pair of computers can only use a single physical line in the port channel at any time but the overall bandwidth of the link is increased using LAG. If many sessions are passing along the LAG, they will be load balanced accordingly.

Configuring Link Aggregation and Control Protocol (LACP) requires two steps. First, a "port channel" must be configured. This is the new logical interface. Second, physical ports must be assigned to this logical interface.

Creating a port channel is very similar to configuring any other interface. Choose a number for your port channel between 1-64, in the example below I am using 11. In this example, the port channel is set up as a trunk port. It can also be set as a routed interface or even as an access port on a single VLAN.

(config)#interface port-channel 11

(config-if)#description "My Port Channel"

(CONFIG-IF)#SWITCHPORT

(config-if)#switchport trunk encap dot1q

(config-if)#switchport mode trunk

(config-if)#switchport trunk allowed vlan 100,110,120,124,130,140,150,160

(config-if)#switchport trunk native vlan 100

(config-if)#no shutdown

After the port channel has been configured, assign physical ports to it. In this case, I am adding two ten gigabit ethernet interfaces to the port channel.

```
(config)#int range te 1/1/3-4
```

```
(config-if)#description "Uplinks"
```

```
(CONFIG-IF)#SWITCHPORT
```

```
(config-if)#channel-group 11 mode on
```

```
(config-if)#no shutdown
```

Now we have two aggregated 10 gbps links for a total bandwidth of 20 gbps. This can help improve throughput and provides redundancy in case of a link failure on one of the lines.

Switch Stack Configuration (StackWise)

Several models of Cisco switches can be configured in "Switch Stacks". These stacks allow multiple physical switches to be combined into one logical unit for control and management.

On some systems proprietary "stackwise" cables like the ones shown below are used to connect multiple switches together. They are wired in typical daisy chain fashion, allowing up to nine members in a single stack. Check the cisco documentation for your model to see the cabling methodology. If any stackwise cable fails the switches can still communicate, but only at half bandwidth.

TIP

For best compatibility, stack members should be the same model and share the same IOS version.

In a switch stack, one unit is elected "master" and performs management tasks for the entire stack. By default, the switch with the lowest MAC address will be elected Master. To manually specify the master the priority value can be changed using the following command. Priority can be between 1 and 15, with 15 being the highest. The highest priority switch will be elected Master.

(config)#switch 1 priority 15

The #show switch command lists the switches currently in the stack, along with their priority value.

Sometimes switches in a stack need to be renumbered. By default, the switches are numbered from lowest to highest MAC address. Because of this, you could end up with switch 3 at the top, switch 1 in the middle, and switch 2 on the bottom of the physical stack! For your own sanity, it's probably easier to have them logically configured the same way they are physically set up.

To renumber a switch, simply execute the following command. In this example, we are changing switch number 1 to switch number 3.

(config)# switch 1 renumber 3

The switch number reassignment takes place after the next reboot.

Virtual Switching System (VSS)

VSS is another system of combining two physical switches into one logical unit. It is available on higher end cisco switches and only supports two switches. Unlike Stackwise both switches must be configured to support it, not just the master. Instead of using Stackwise cables typical copper or fiber ethernet connections are used to make the connection between the units.

Like with Stackwise, when using VSS you can create LAGs (port channel's) across two switches. This allows you to have redundancy that would otherwise not be possible. Without VSS, links to one switch would be put into blocking mode by STP. In this scenario links to both switches can pass traffic at the same time, and if a physical switch fails you can ensure you still have connectivity as long as your downstream equipment is physically cabled to both VSS switches.

To configure VSS, you must first assign both units to the same Virtual Domain. In the virtual domain section, you must also assign a number to the switch, such as Switch 1 for the first and Switch 2 for the second. On the interface that will be connecting the units together (A port-channel, in the example below) you must enter the (config-if)#switch virtual link 1 command. Lastly, the stitches must be converted to VSS mode using the (config)#switch convert mode virtual command. After the command has been executed, the switches will reboot and they will act as one logical unit!

To return the switches to stand alone units, use the (config)#switch convert mode stand-alone command.

TIP

Configuration can only be done from the primary switch, so make sure you are consoling into the primary when making configuration changes. The standby console will prevented from making any configuration changes.

VSS Lab

Switch 1 Configuration

S1(config)#switch virtual domain 100

S1(config-vs-domain)#switch 1

!

S1(config)#interface port-channel 1

S1(config-if)#switchport

S1(config-if)#switch virtual link 1

S1(config-if)#no shutdown

S1(config-if)#exit

!

S1(config)#int range te 1/13-16

S1(config-if-range)#description "VSS Link"

S1(config-if-range)#channel-group 1 mode on

S1(config-if-range)#no shutdown

!

S1(config)#switch convert mode virtual

Switch 2 Configuration

S2(config)#switch virtual domain 100

S2(config-vs-domain)#switch 2

!

S2(config)#interface port-channel 2

S2(config-if)#switchport

S2(config-if)#switch virtual link 2

S2(config-if)#no shutdown

S2(config-if)#exit

!

S2(config)#int range te 1/13-16

S2(config-if-range)#description "VSS Link"

S2(config-if-range)#channel-group 2 mode on

S2(config-if-range)#no shutdown

!

S2(config)#switch convert mode virtual

To view the status of the VSS, you can use the #show switch virtual command which shows you information about the active and standby switches.

<u>TO RELOAD BOTH SWITCHES AT ONCE USE THE</u> (config)#redundancy reload shelf command. You can also choose to reload only the peer, if required. The normal reload command will only reload the primary unit, causing the second switch to be promoted to active.

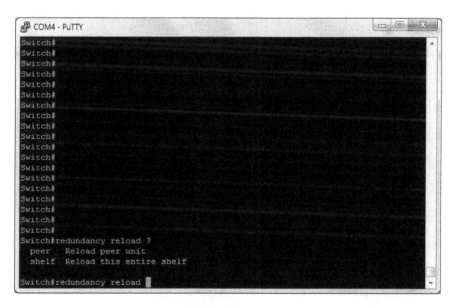

Chapter 10 The OSI and TCP/IP models

Since the establishment of the reference models like OSI and TCP/IP various illustrations were published to describe simply and accurately the communication process between two computers in a LAN or the Internet. That said, the following sections will provide brief explanations about the working principle of the two well-known reference models such TCP/IP and OSI.

TCP/IP Reference Model

When considering the fact that communication between two computers consists of certain segments and that these segments in the world of computer networks according to reference models are called layers of communication, then it will not be that hard to understand the layered nature of the TCP/IP reference model. Therefore, to not confuse the TCP and IP protocols with the TCP/IP reference model, we consider the fact that the TCP/IP reference model is a set of protocols where IP and TCP protocols are dominant. In Figure 1 the communication process in TCP/IP reference model is shown.

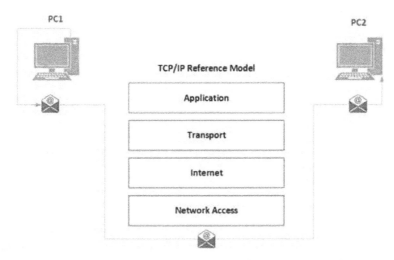

Figure 1. Communication in TCP/IP Reference Model

In each layer operates a significant number of protocols. Some of the most used protocols in the layers of TCP/IP reference model are as follows:

·   Application Layer – operate protocols such as telnet, FTP, SMTP, DNS, RIP, and others.

·   Transport Layer – operate protocols such as TCP and UDP.

·   Internet Layer – operate protocols such as IP, ARP, IGMP, and ICMP.

·   Network Access Layer – operate communication technologies such as Ethernet, Token Ring, Frame Relay and ATM.

Thus, when viewing the communication process between two computers from the perspective of the TCP/IP reference model the following takes place:

·   Software application interacts with the Application Layer - Depending on the type of software used an interaction is established with a proper protocol in the application layer. Once the request of an application to communicate in the network has been processed by the relevant protocol in the application layer, the same request by the same protocol is sent further in the layer below to the relevant protocols.

·   HTTP protocol from an Application Layer interacts with the TCP protocol in the Transport Layer – TCP takes care to package the data coming from HTTP into segments called Datagram and forwards it to IP protocol in the Internet Layer so that these datagrams of data are transmitted to the destination. The IP protocol, adds the logical elements such as IP source and IP destination on the received TCP datagram thus the data becomes a packet. Thereafter, packets are transmitted to the lower layer of the TCP/IP reference model.

Practice proves that, today, is the Ethernet the communication technology that is widely used in the local area networks (LAN) thus protocols like LLC, MAC and physical (electrical signals) come into play. In this layer, packets coming from the Internet layer will be organized in the frames and as such will be carried over to the network equipment and then to the router in order to transmit the data through the Internet further to its destination.

OSI Reference Model

Thus, the OSI reference model enabled a detailed description of the hardware and software components involved in the communication process among computers. This approach represents the strict approach to layers of OSI reference model compared with that of TCP/IP reference model. The Figure 2 shows the communication process in OSI reference model.

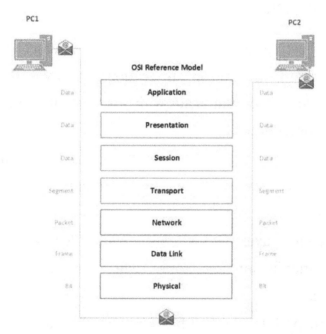

Figure 2. Communication in OSI Reference Model

To better understand the working principle of the OSI reference model, let's take the example of the assembly line in the automobile factory. As we have seen it in TV documentaries or told by a friend who works in the factory, everything starts from the chassis (or frame), which is placed as the first element in the assembly line. At each step of an assembly, one or more elements (or parts) of the vehicle are placed. After a considerable number of steps, at the end of the assembly line a brand new vehicle comes out which is then sent for testing.

Almost the same happens in the OSI reference model when it comes to describing a communication session between two computers. In each layer of OSI a certain activity is assigned that prepares the data for the subsequent layer.

- Application layer - is responsible to interact with the operating system or application whenever the user decides to communicate with his computer through a computer network.
- Presentation layer - receives data from the application layer and represents them in the format accepted by the subsequent layer.
- Session layer – is responsible for establishing communication sessions whenever needed (on-demand).
- Transport layer - the fact that on this layer the TCP protocol operates, then this layer adds the credibility, order of transmission, and control for errors in data transmission.
- Network layer – logical elements such as IP addresses and routing protocols take place in this layer.

- Data link layer – is responsible for assigning the physical protocols dependable upon the communication technology used in LANs.
- Physical layer – represents both the physical and logical aspects of computer network. Among the physical components are network interface card (NIC), the medium for data transmission, and the network equipment; while among logical components are electrical signals and transmission time.

Whether you're talking about the theoretical approach of communication in a computer networks that is OSI reference model, or about the practical approach of communication in a computer networks that is TCP/IP reference model, the two together continue to be the reference models for description and implementation of the communication in computer networks. Also, despite the fact that communication technologies have advanced, the IPv6 addressing is being implemented, that the Internet2, the Internet of Things and the Internet of Everything and more or less just some of the efforts to improve and advance the current Internet; regardless in the field of description and implementation of communication in computer networks both OSI and TCP/IP reference models remain intact!

Chapter 11 The IP addresses and subnets

Once upon the time...

Decades ago, it all began as a need for data communication, or rather as a need for "sharing" the resources between computers. Years later, in 1974 Vinton G. Cerf and Robert E. Kahn through a research paper proposed the primary protocols to be used for the communication on the ARPANET. Always according to them, this set of protocols would be called TCP/IP and will consist of TCP protocol (operating in transport layer of the OSI model) and IP protocol (operating in network layer of the OSI model). That led to a birth of the Internet protocol TCP/IP, the initial specification of which will pass through four versions to reach the climax with the fourth version IPv4 in 1979. Nearly a decade from the time it appeared, the fourth version of the TCP/IP was standardized through the ARPANET's Request for Comments (RFC) documents.

IP Addresses

IPv4 addressing technology, as noted above, is the fourth version of the IP addresses. In brief, IPv4 address or just IP address is a logical element that consists of 32 bits and for the purposes of easier interpretation is organized into four groups of 8 bits split by point. So, considering that 1 byte = 8 bits, then an IP address is 4 bytes where each group of 8 bits represents 1 byte. That said, since the binary numerical system represents the machine language which computers understand, then the total number of IPv4 addresses is 4,294,967,296. If compared with the current number of inhabitants on our planet, then obviously, it's missing nearly 3 billion IP addresses. That's why the IPv6 addressing technology has been introduced.

The Internet Corporation for Assigned Names and Numbers (ICANN) organization is responsible for assigning the IP addresses. Thus, to ease the process of assigning IP addresses the IP address classes were introduced. In each IP address there's a representation of the network and the host portion.

Sub-networks

One of the reasons why one would subnet a computer network is to implement multiple logical networks within existing classes like A, B, and C. Also, subnet mask plays an important role in determining the size of the network. Then, by definition subnet mask is a 32-bit address used in combination with an IP address to indicate the network and its computers. Each class has a default subnet mask. The Figure 3 shows the default subnet masks of each class of IP addresses.

Subnet Mask	Network	Host	Host	Host
Class A	255	0	0	0
Class B	255	255	0	0
Class C	255	255	255	0

Figure 2. Default subnet masks

Today, the information accessed on the Internet is provided through IPv4-based infrastructure. Despite shortcomings like the lack of public IP addresses or in regard to security, IPv4 continues to serve users across the globe. Despite the forecasts, time will tell whether the IPv4 addressing will remain a choice and the right solution for the next generation of computer networks!

Chapter 12 IPv6

What are the benefits of using IPv6?

One thing we can always guarantee in life is that "CHANGE" will always happen. It's just inevitable...(i.e.: our bodies change as we get older, our relationships change as time goes by, our jobs and titles change as companies implement new technologies, the CCNA certification exam changed from the (640-802) to the new one you will take now, the (200-120)...see, everything changes) However, some of us resist change. That is what I like to call TCRS or "The Change Resistance Syndrome" ...here you go Wikipedia – add that to your list!

I saw this happen when we were going from NT4 to NT5 which was WIN2K, (if you are a millennial, then most likely you do not know what that is; this is meant for the dinosaurs in the room). Wow! We dreaded that change, didn't we? We thought that nothing could improve NT4 right?...WRONG! I remember the complaints and the resistance to change then as I still see the resistance now; not just from employees either, but also from employers. TCRS was entrenched back then as it is today. I know it's difficult, but hey, you must adapt and overcome this fear of change. After all, you can't stop it, so you might as well embrace it, or at least try. If you listen to the naysayers, you know, those that will try to convince you that there are NO new benefits to IPv6 then you will be lost, confused, aggravated and stressed out. Why put yourself through the ringer about something that is inevitable and ultimately simple to learn. So, to those individuals out there, and believe me, you will encounter plenty; I want you to respond in an informed and competent manner, and let them know that YES, there are plenty of benefits to switching to IPv6. I want you to then proceed to point out the benefits that IPv6 brings; for example: we have IPsec built in that provides end to end security, a header that is half the size of IPv4, and since its aligned to 64 bits, it will increase the processing speed significantly as well. Of course we know the awe-inspiring number of IP's that would now allow for more efficient routing, and let's not forget the new types of addresses such as "Anycast" known also as "One to Nearest", and hallelujah...no more BROADCAST! It is all now "Multicast" and you could have many different types of addresses on the same interface; Unicast, Multicast, and Anycast. I know what you're thinking. "Man, this is awesome!" YES IT IS!

I would of course like to mention the Link-local address, but that will always be present on your PC regardless of DHCP or not; this will be present on your router's interface as well. Just wanted to throw that out there just as an FYI.☐

So, mark my words, IPv6 is chalk full of benefits and enhancements that will be most advantageous to us all.

The assignment of these addresses are different as well, let me explain; we could assign the IP address statically, both the Network Prefix and Interface ID, followed by its prefix-length, or we could just put the network prefix portion of the address followed by a double colon and ending it with the prefix-length, whatever it may be.

In order to generate the Interface ID portion of it, we would use another new feature called auto-configuration which is typing this command: eui-64 after the prefix length. It will generate the Interface ID portion of the address using the MAC address of the routers interface. That will only give us a 48 bit address. But hey!...we need 64 bits. So, to accommodate for the missing bits, it will pad the MAC address with the following: FFFE to the middle of the address, meaning it will insert the FFFE smack in the middle of the MAC address to make it 64 bits.

So, most definitely IPv6 brings its benefits; this is but a nibble of all the benefits it brings. But it's enough for what we need to know for certification purposes and employment needs for now.

Now, let's start looking at these addresses and how they are made-up.

Addressing and Expressions

Remember IPv6 addresses are in hexadecimal format, and they are separated into 8 sections of 4 hexadecimal numbers separated by colons. This creates our 128 bit address.

Example:

2001:3200:0abc: 1100:0000:0000:1234:abc1/64

Do not let the size of this address deter you from your goal! We will dissect this type of address and understand what we are looking at, to include the make-up of this 128 bit address.

An IPv6 address is really broken into two parts, the first part is made up of four (4) sections. This part is called the Network Prefix. The next part also has four (4) sections and is called the Interface ID. The 2nd part of the address (Interface ID), can be generated automatically using the eui-64 command. The /64 is also called the prefix-length, this is NOT a subnetmask as it was in IPv4.

FYI: *The word CIDR is use in IPv4 only and is therefore considered an archaic terminology. This is used for routing purposes only and it has nothing to do with the Interface ID of the address.*

Let us breakdown the above address into its two parts and then further breakdown each section of the Network Prefix portion of the address as follows:

2001	3200	0abc	1100	0000	0000	1234	abc1
Network Prefix 64 Bits				Interface ID 64 Bits			

Once again remember that the values you are looking at are hexadecimal values! Each one of those numbers or letters really represents 4 bits...you didn't forget, did you? You need to understand that, this is how each section equates to 16 bits.

Now let's take the Network Prefix and place each section into its category:

118

2001	3200	0abc	1100
Registry	ISP	Company	Subnet

In IPv6 we do not have "Classes" of addresses. What we do have in IPv6 is designation of addresses.

Let's consider the figure above...this is an example of a Global Unicast address. How do we know this? Well, this is simple. You should immediately recognize this by just looking at the first section of the address. Global Unicast addresses starts with 2001. This means that you need to be able to look at an IPv6 address and be able to snap your fingers and know what type of address it is without dwelling too much on it. Take my word for it, this will become second nature to you as you practice and read this``5earlie a few times.

If the address would have started with FE80, then you would have known that the IPv6 address would be considered a Link-local address instead. So in order to identify an IPv6 address we would look at the first section of the network prefix.

We will take a look at the different types of addresses further in this book.

Isn't this address just too big to type every time you need it? It certainly is! We need to make things fast and simple in order to be able to spend our precious time doing other things rather than typing these 128 bit addresses over and over again. "Is there a shorter method to these addresses? Thank goodness there is! "The powers that be" must have read our minds and actually thought the same thing. They came up with a fantastic way to shorten the expression and alleviate our fingers in the process. However, like everything in IT, it has rules that must be followed:

Rules

1. There can only be one (1) set of double colons- NO EXCEPTIONS

2. You can only remove leading zeroes from the address.

3. The complete address must equate to eight sections.

4. You can only go up to F in the hex table. *"This one is just common sense"*.

Using the same address let's see how we can shorten it.

2001:3200:0abc:1100:0000:0000:1234:abc1/64

(Numbers highlighted in red can be removed.)

2001:3200:abc:1100::1234:abc1/64

We have removed all leading zeroes and the two sets of contiguous zeroes by using one double colon, this is a valid IPv6 address.

So what would an invalid IPv6 address look like?

Here is an example:

2001::HE35::1569:BEEF

The address above is breaking all the rules isn't it? First we have 2 sets of double colons, you should know that only one (1) set of double colons is permitted. So, why is that wrong? First of all, the protocol would not know where to place the zeroes, and secondly, hex numbers don not go beyond the letter "F". In this example, we see the letter "H" in the address, and it looks like we only have 6 sections instead of eight, but that could be due to the double colons that represent consecutive zeroes right? None the less, the above address is invalid one way or another and cannot be used.

Recognizing a valid & invalid address is extremely important when taking your certification exam. I do not want you to get points taken off for something as simple as this.

FYI: *You can have upper case and lower case hex in the address (as the examples above indicate), it does NOT make a difference as far as configuration is concerned...it is a matter of preference. Having said that, Cisco recommends that you keep the hex letters in lower case. In this book I do both. The upper case is mainly to make a visual emphasis. But, again, please follow the rules and do what Cisco recommends, why be defiant? After all, you need to get your CCNA.*

If asked, how can we fix this invalid address? Well, let's give it a try shall we?

2001:0:CE35:0:1569:BEEF::1

Here, I added a zero were the double colons were. From there on I had no idea about the rest of the address. Therefore, I simply put a double colon to represent a section of zeros, and ended the address with a 1, which in turn would give us the Interface ID portion of the address to complete the eight sections needed. I also took the "H" and replaced it with a "C"...which is now a true value in the hex table to make this address valid.

Again, I did this to show the difference between a valid IPv6 address and an invalid IPv6 address to drive the message that, you need to recognize the difference between the two.

Expect to be asked the difference between valid & an invalid IPv6 address in the Cisco certification exam.

Statically Assigning addresses

Assigning IPv6 addresses to a router is pretty much the same thing as in IPv4; but instead of typing IP address:

192.168.1.1 255.255.255.0

You would type IPv6 address:
2001:3200:0abc:1100:0000:0000:1234:abc1/64.

However, try using the shortened expression wherever possible, meaning, get rid of the leading zeroes and all consecutive zeroes were possible. Learning this will make your life a whole lot easier...and remember that you will learn it with practice.

When using IPv6, there is no need to type "IPv6 enable" on the interface unless you want to specifically use the Link-local address only. Once you type-in the complete address manually, it will enable IPv6.

CAUTION! Doing this command will not enable routing of the IPv6 addresses. Confused? Don't worry, we will talk about that later on.

Using the EUI-64

Another way you could assign IPv6 addresses is by using the eui-64 command. This works by generating the Interface ID portion of the address automatically. It uses the MAC address of the interface to perform this task. "But wait Laz, that's only 48 bits - we need 64" There's a simple explanation to this as well. Let me explain; what eui-64 does in order to make it a 64 bit address is to PAD or insert an FFFE in-between the MAC address.

The main concern here should be with your MAC address being part of the IPv6 complete address. But if your security is in place, (...and it better be if you care about your job), then you should have nothing to worry about. You should only be concerned with two things; "what does the command do? And how to configure it.

The following is an example of using the eui-64 command:

The following output would be the result of using the eui-64 command.

DHCPv6

Well DHCP is pretty much DHCP; whether it's IPv4 or IPv6. It still does what it knows how to do best - lease addresses. Obviously we need to understand that we are now doing it for IPv6. Nonetheless, there are still a few limitations within the IOS of a Cisco router for DHCPv6; including DHCPv6 stateless support.

Know this, DHCP servers will be around for a bit. They are not going to disappear just yet so you must make sure you are still up to date when it comes to setting one up.

In my very humble opinion, I would shy away from setting up a router with the DHCP service enabled. My reasoning behind this is simply due to broadcasting to lease an address and also because of the continuous renewal of that address. I believe routers have more important tasks to perform than assigning IP addresses. But hey...that's me!

You can always set it up as a Relay Agent, using the IP-helper command on an interface, so it can go on behalf of the client to an actual DHCP server and have an IP address assigned to the client.

Yet again...no one should be going across broadcast domains to have IP address assigned to them; most specifically if it's across a WAN. The only way I can justify turning a router into a DHCP server is, if it's a small company. And even then, I have my reservations on that.

Chapter 13 Wireless Technology Security

In the previous chapter, I listed security threat as one of the most dangerous challenges of computer networking. This is not unconnected to the havoc that potential cybercriminals can wreck on a network with lax security measures. In this chapter, I will discuss the concept of wireless technology security extensively in order to assist you to have a deeper understanding of the concept, the potential security threats, and the practical security tips that can serve as preventive measures against these threats.

What is wireless network security?

This is the first question that most people ask. Well, there are different definitions for wireless network security. According to Wikipedia, "wireless security is the prevention of unauthorized access or damage to computers using wireless networks."

This definition by Technopedia also captures the concept well: "Wireless network security is the process of designing, implementing, and ensuring security on a wireless computer network. It is a subset of network security that adds protection for a wireless computer network."

These two definitions have obviously given you a better understanding of wireless network security that is otherwise known as wireless security. Wireless security is designed to protect a wireless network form malicious access attempts by potential hackers as well as from unauthorized personnel. Going by the name, you will realize that wireless network security is also done with a wireless switch/router or other wireless devices that by default can encrypt and secure wireless communication.

Sometimes, the wireless security may be compromised. In that event, the hacker is prevented from viewing the content of the packet or traffic in transit. More so, there are wireless intrusion systems that are responsible for detecting potential intrusions and preventing such an intrusion by alerting the network administrator whenever it detects any security breach.

Types of wireless network security

The increased global concern about the security of wireless networks has triggered the need for different security measures to be developed with the goal of reinforcing the security of wireless networks. Wireless network security can be achieved through some standards and algorithms that are specifically designed for that purpose. Some of these security measures are:

Wi-Fi Protected Access (WPA)

The Wi-Fi Protected Access is a security certification and security program for securing wireless computer networks designed to address some of the weaknesses in the Wired Equivalent Privacy (WEP). When you use WPA encryption for securing your Wi-Fi networks, you need a passphrase, otherwise known as a password, or a network security key. The passphrases are usually made up of numbers and letters. To establish a connection to the Wi-Fi network, the computer and whatever other connected devices must use the passphrase.

If you personally own the Wi-Fi network, it is advisable that you choose your own password when setting up the Wi-Fi network. Your password must be lengthy and be made up of alphanumeric characters and special characters to increase the security level of the password to prevent someone without the right authorization access to your network. When choosing a passphrase, you should also ensure that your passphrase is unique and cannot be easily guessed or cracked.

Wired Equivalent Policy (WEP)

WEP has been around for years. It's one of the security methods that have been around for years, especially for supporting older devices. The WEP security technique is not difficult to implement. You will trigger a network security key whenever you enable the WEP. The security key will encrypt any information that the computer shares with any other computer on the network. WEP was made known to the public by the Institute of Electrical and Electronics Engineers (IEEE) in 1979. This is a not-for-profit organization that has the responsibility of developing the right standards that can be adopted in electronic transmissions. There are two types of WEP. They are:

- *Shared key authentication:* This is a channel through which a computer can access a WEP-based wireless network. If a computer has a wireless modem, SKA will allow it to have access to the WEP network to enable it to exchange both unencrypted and encrypted data. For this authentication type to function efficiently, a wireless access point must match a WEP encryption key that has been obtained prior to the time of use by the connecting computer.

The connection process starts when the computer contacts the access point with an authentication request. In response to the request, the access point will generate a challenge text, a sequence of characters, for the computer. The computer will use its WEP key for encrypting the challenge text and later transmit it to the access point. After receiving the message, the access point will decrypt it and subsequently compare the result of the decrypted message with the main challenge text. If there are no mistakes in the decrypted message, the access point will immediately send the authentication code needed by the connecting computer to the computer. Then, finally, the connecting computer will accept the sent authentication code and thus is integrated into the network throughout the session or throughout the period when the connecting computer is within the original access point's range.

On the other hand, if there is a discrepancy between the original text and the decrypted message, the access point will prevent the computer from becoming a part of the network.

- *Open system authentication:* The Open System Authentication (OSA) refers to a technique that allows a computer to gain unrestricted access to a WEP-based wireless network. With this system authentication, any computer that has a wireless modem can gain access to any network where it can receive unencrypted files. For the Open System Authentication to work, the computer's Service Set Identifier (SSID) should be the same with that of the wireless access point. The SSID refers to some well-arranged characters that uniquely assign names to a Wireless Local Area Network. The whole process occurs in just three stages.

First, the computer will send a request to the access point for authentication. When the access point receives the request, it will randomly generate an authentication code that is intended for use at the right time: during the session. Finally, the computer will take the authentication code and thus integrate into the network throughout the duration of the session and as long as the computer is within the range of the access point. You need a Shared Key Authentication (SKA), a better and stronger authentication technique, if you find it necessary to transfer encrypted data between a wireless-equipped computer and the access point of a WEP network.

Top ways to secure your wireless network

Today, the popularity of wireless networks comes at a price: cybercriminals are always on the lookout for possible loopholes they can exploit to breach your security and compromise your data. Hence, it is a matter of urgency to find some ways to beef the security of your wireless network to prevent these criminals from breaching your security. Here are some security measures that can guarantee the security of your wireless network:

Understand the principle behind wireless networks

Understanding the principle behind how a wireless network works can be of help in safeguarding your wireless networks. If you want to go wireless, you need to connect a DSL modem, a cable, or any other access point to a wireless router. The router will then send a signal out through the air to the desired destination, which may sometimes be a couple of hundred feet away. Any device that is connected within the range will be able to pull the signal and have access to the Internet. With this understanding, you are likely more willing to take necessary precautions to ensure that no one has access to your network besides yourself and other authorized people.

Encrypt your wireless network

If you are using a wireless network at home or in your office, make it a point of duty to encrypt any type of information you want to transfer over the network to prevent eavesdroppers from gaining access to your confidential information. When you encrypt a data, it is scrambled into a code that others cannot gain access to. Encrypting your data is obviously the most potent way of shutting out intruders from your network.

There are two encryption techniques for the encryption: WPA and WEP. You should always use the same encryption for your router, computer, and other devices. If you need ideas, give WPA2 a try. This encryption technique is efficient and will secure your network against hackers. If you use wireless routers, they always have their encryption turned off. Turn this feature on to secure your network. You will find how to do this if you go through the router's manual. If you can't find the instruction on the manual, visit the router company's official website for the instruction.

Limit access to your network

It is also your responsibility to ensure that only certain devices are allowed to access your wireless network. All the devices that are able to effectively communicate with a wireless network are automatically assigned a unique MAC (Media Access Control) address. Wireless routers are designed with a mechanism that they use for allowing devices that have specific MAC address to gain access to a network to ensure the security of your network.

However, you should be cautious when using this security option. Some hackers and other cybercriminals have found a way to mimic MAC addresses and can easily infiltrate your network. Therefore, complement this security technique with some other effective network security techniques.

Secure your router

Your router is another device that deserves protection as well so that your wireless network won't be susceptible to cyber-attack via some loopholes in the security of your router. It is the responsibility of your router to direct traffic between the Internet and your local network. Therefore, protecting your router is the first step towards the protection of your entire network. If you leave your router unprotected, strangers may gain access to your network and thus access your personal and confidential information such as your financial information. If they have complete control of your router, you can't predict what they will do with your network.

Change your router's default name

Your router obviously comes with a default name. This name is sometimes called SSID or the service set identifier. This is the name assigned to the router by the manufacturer. To increase the security of your wireless network, it is advisable that you change this default name and give the router a unique and difficult-to-guess name. Also, don't reveal this name to anyone. If you are the only person with access to the default name, it is almost impossible for the router to be subjected to a security breach.

Change the router's default password(s)

Just as the router comes with a default name, it also comes with a default password or a group of passwords. This password gives you the freedom to set up the router as well as operate it. Hackers are familiar with the default passwords and can use the knowledge to hack your router and gain access to your network if you leave the default password(s) unchanged. Make the password change for both the "administrator" and "user."

The rule of thumb stipulates that you use a combination of letters and numbers, known as alphanumeric characters, as well as long and difficult-to-guess passwords. It is advisable that you use a minimum of 12 characters for your password. You may also include lowercase and uppercase letters. The more complex your password, the more difficult it is for hackers to break. If you are unsure about how to change the password, visit the router company's website, and you will be guided through the process.

Don't always log in as administrator

After you have successfully set up your router, don't keep yourself logged in as administrator. Rather, you should log out immediately if you are not using the router. This will reduce the risk of being piggybacked on during your session in order to have access to your login details and take control of your router. That may have a dire consequence on your network.

Turn off "Remote Management" features

The reason for this security measure is pretty obvious. Some routers' manufacturers offer the option to keep the remote management option turned on in order to provide you with technical support when necessary. Sadly, leaving this option turned on is synonymous to making your financial information available to the public. Hackers may capitalize on the feature to gain access to your router and, invariably, your network. On the other hand, when you leave this feature turned off, controlling your network from a remote location is impossible.

Always update your router

In order for your router to work effectively and be secure, the accompanying software must be regularly updated to fix bugs and other issues. Before setting up your router, visit the router's website to see if you can get the updated software that you can download. It is a course of wisdom to register the router with the manufacturer as well as sign up to receive regular updates to ensure that you are kept in the loop whenever there is a new software version.

Secure your computer

Regardless of the security measures you adopt for your router and other devices that are connected to your network, it is imperative that you secure your computer too. For instance, you can use some protections such as antispyware, antivirus, and firewall to fortify the security of your computer. Remember to keep the software up-to-date as well. Some valuable security tips include using a strong password for your computer and using up-to-date antivirus, antispyware, and firewalls. Don't forget to enable 2-factor authentication as well. Read this article: "**Computer Security**" for more practical tips that will help you keep your computer safe and secure from potential cybercriminals.

Log out of connected apps

If you access your network via an app, don't keep the app open when you are not using the app. Log out immediately and log in again whenever you want to access the network with the app. Why should you go through this process of logging in and out frequently? Remember that you can lose your phone or have it stolen at any time. Keeping the app open allows others to access your network via the stolen or lost phone. To further increase the security of the network through the app, adopt the password tips. Use a strong password that hackers will have a challenging time hacking so the chances of others gaining access to your network through your app are drastically reduced.

Password your phone

While password-protecting your app is a good idea, think about making your phone inaccessible to others as well. Protecting your phone will create the first barrier against unauthorized access to your phone and your network. I have given a list of practical tips for creating strong and difficult-to-hack passwords. Go through the chapter again and implement the tips. The stronger your password, the more difficult it is to hack your phone and access sensitive information that may be used against you or your network.

Reduce the range of your wireless signal

This is another effective security option you should consider. This is applicable to users whose wireless routers have a very high range while the users are using small spaces for operation. If you are in that group, decrease the signal range. There are two ways to do this. You can either change your wireless channel or change your router's mode to 802.11g rather than the conventional 802.11b or 802.11n. Alternatively, you can place the router in some secluded places such as inside a shoe box or under a bed. You can also wrap a foil around its antennas to perfectly restrict its signals' direction.

Stay under the radar

To hide the visibility of your network and stop your wireless network from broadcasting its presence, disable the router's Service Set Identifier (SSID) to make it "invisible." This will prevent strangers beside your business or home from being aware of the network and its name. This will also reduce the number of people who may be interested in gaining access to your network.

Turn off the network when not in use

This is considered by some experts as "the ultimate in wireless security measures." The reason for this assertion is not far-fetched: if you shut your network down, most hackers will certainly be prevented from breaking in. While it may be impractical to keep switching the network off and on frequently, it is still practical to do it occasionally when you won't be using the network for a long time, perhaps when on vacation or when you will be offline for an extended period of time.

Have antimalware installed on connected devices

It is not out of place to take an inventory of the wide variety of devices connected to the network. When you have a full list of the devices, ensure that they all have antimalware installed on each of the devices for maximum protection against external invasion, especially in devices that can support the protection. Listed above are some effective ways you can close the door to your wireless network to the bad guys and thus prevent your network from being compromised. The suggestions here are practical and very easy to implement.

The tips discussed above have been tested and proven reliable over the years. Since precaution is usually better than cure, taking these steps to boost the security of your network is more rewarding and more effective than waiting until disaster strikes before running from pillar to post looking for a solution to the problem, so increase the immunity of your network and give cybercriminals a second thought about making attempts to breach your security. If you don't implement these tips, you are a sitting duck, an easy target for hackers.

Conclusion

Technology has gradually transitioned from wired to wireless over the years with tons of benefits. From the Internet of Things to wireless communication, we are all eyewitnesses of the huge benefits of wireless technologies. However, it doesn't come without some challenges, too, primarily, security issues. This book has covered all these subjects extensively and has highlighted both the benefits and challenges of wireless technologies. It has also given us an insight into what the world stands to gain from wireless technologies in the future. These are salient points that keep reminding us of what the world holds for us. It is imperative that you and I take full advantage of these technologies and use them to the full. That's one of the ways we can enjoy life to the fullest; we have the technologies to get things done better, faster, and easier.

www.ingramcontent.com/pod-product-compliance
Lightning Source LLC
Chambersburg PA
CBHW071140050326
40690CB00008B/1521